Webster's

Kikuyu

–

English

Thesaurus Dictionary

PROCEEDS BENEFIT

Webster's Online Dictionary
(www.websters-online-dictionary.org)

EDITED BY

Philip M. Parker, Ph.D.
INSEAD (Fontainebleau & Singapore)

Published by ICON Group International, Inc.
7404 Trade St
San Diego, CA 92122 USA
Phone: (858) 635-9410
Fax: (858) 635-9414
iconsubs@san.rr.com

www.icongrouponline.com

This edition published by ICON Classics in 2008
Printed in the United States of America.

Webster's Kikuyu – English Thesaurus Dictionary

ISBN 0-497-83548-7

PREFACE

This is an English thesaurus designed for Kikuyu speakers who wish to better understand the ambiguities and richness of the English language. The first chapter is a full English thesaurus organized by 871 Kikuyu subject words. For each Kikuyu subject word, one or more corresponding English subject words (translations) are provided. Synonyms are then given for the English translations for all relevant parts of speech (even in cases where the Kikuyu subject word has a unique part of speech). This process results in over 10355 English synonyms.

The second chapter gives an index of these English synonyms back to the Kikuyu subject words (a potentially useful chapter to English speakers interested in basic Kikuyu vocabulary). The third chapter has short vocabulary lists organized by parts-of-speech. English teachers or students can use these bilingual lists to create flash cards, basic lesson plans, and English as a Second Language (ESL) study lists.

While creating an English thesaurus for Kikuyu speakers seems simple enough, it can be tricky. What's the problem? Translations do not always follow strict transitivity. Normally, if $a=b$ and $b=c$, then $c=a$. This is not necessarily true in linguistics when b is an English word that has more than one part of speech. For example, "test" is a verb, noun and adjective. What is the correct English synonym for "a" (in Kikuyu) when "b" (in English) has synonyms ("c") having many parts of speech? Furthermore, what if "a" (in Kikuyu) is ambiguous and has several translations into English ("b")? This thesaurus embraces this ambiguity by giving as much information to the reader as possible. This was accomplished in two phases. In the first phase, maximum-likelihood English translations of the Kikuyu subject words are given. For all the languages covered in Webster's Online Dictionary translations are determined using rather massive content analyses of translations from various sources including translations of United Nations documents, translations of the Holy Bible (and similar sources), training manuals, popular works, and academic sources. An English translation having the highest probability of being used is reported first, then the second most probable is reported second, and so on.

Reference: Webster's Online Dictionary (www.websters-online-dictionary.org)

In the second phase, English synonyms for all parts of speech, including those not related to the original Kikuyu subject, are given for each English translation generated by the first phase. If an English entry is most used as a certain part of speech (estimated based on an English language corpus), then English synonyms for that part of speech are listed first. This indicates to the speaker of Kikuyu how the English subject word is most used. Other parts of speech are listed based on their frequency of usage in English. Within each part of speech, synonyms most likely to be used in English are listed first. Readers who seek further information on any of the words in this book, including translations to other world languages, can freely refer to Webster's Online Dictionary (www.websters-online-dictionary.org).

The goal of Webster's Online Dictionary is to give all people of the world free access to a complete mapping of all known words to and from all written languages. In fulfillment of this goal, Webster's Online Dictionary (www.websters-online-dictionary.org) also offers as much information as possible for each word, including definitions, translations, images, trade name usage, quotations, and encyclopedic knowledge. The proceeds generated by the sale of this Kikuyu–English thesaurus dictionary as well as other books extracted from the project will be used to augment the contents of the Webster's Online Dictionary.

This book may be the first Kikuyu-English thesaurus ever published. All the errors and omissions are mine. I will certainly revise and improve this book at some later date, so if you wish to see better editions published in the future, please send any suggestions, corrections, or translations to webstersedits2@hotmail.com. Thank you for purchasing this book and supporting Webster's Online Dictionary.

Philip M. Parker, Ph.D., editor
Chair Professor of Management Science
INSEAD (Singapore & Fontainebleau, France)

CONTENTS

Kikuyu to English Thesaurus

A

agana wicked; *synonyms* (*adj*) atrocious, bad, evil, sinful, vicious, depraved, immoral, mischievous, unholy, vile, corrupt, criminal, diabolical, foul, hellish, iniquitous, nasty, naughty, pernicious, ungodly, impious, perverse, base, black, dark, despicable, devilish, diabolic, disgusting, dissolute; *antonyms* (*adj*) good, innocent, kind, moral, pious, pure.

agIrIra 1. befit; *synonyms* (*v*) suit, become, beseem, fit, pertain, sit, (*adj*) behoove, meet, **2**. suit; *synonyms* (*n*) lawsuit, plea, action, case, petition, cause, courtship, prayer, outfit, request, gear, appeal, entreaty, (*v*) agree, correspond, accommodate, adapt, answer, match, please, adjust, satisfy, accord, befit, harmonize, square, conform, serve, do, set.

aka 1. construct; *synonyms* (*v*) make, build, compose, erect, fabricate, form, arrange, constitute, manufacture, produce, raise, rear, assemble, compile, create, fashion, shape, fabric, organize, cause, contrive, craft, design, devise, do, establish, forge, (*n*) concept, conception, notion; *antonyms* (*v*) destroy, demolish, **2**. put together; *synonyms* (*v*) combine, construct, join, prepare, frame, weave, incorporate, mix, configure, connect, edify, piece, place, (*adv*) collectively, conjointly, jointly, **3**. build; *synonyms* (*v*) rise, base, found, formulate, calculate, increase, rely, (*n*) construction, figure, built, conformation, constitution, cut, formation, physique, set, stature, structure, anatomy, body.

akia mundia heap up; *synonyms* (*v*) amass, accumulate, gather, pile, collect, compile, load.

ambata 1. climb; *synonyms* (*v*) ascend, arise, clamber, escalate, increase, scale, scramble, lift, bestride, fly, (*n*) rise, mount, ascent, acclivity, advance, ascending, jump, ascension, climbing, hike, mounting, raise, upgrade, ramble; *antonyms* (*v*) descend, drop, **2**. ascend; *synonyms* (*v*) climb, uprise, appear, soar.

amUkIra receive; *synonyms* (*v*) accept, admit, get, assume, adopt, bear, have, obtain, welcome, make, acknowledge, embrace, gather, greet, take, hear, earn, own, realize, derive, entertain, include, absorb, acquire, capture, catch, collect, comprehend, contain, deliver.

anaina shiver; *synonyms* (*n*) quiver, fragment, splinter, thrill, chill, frisson, tremor, palpitation, vibration, fright, (*v*) shake, tremble, quake, shudder, palpitate, shatter, tingle, crash, dither, smash, flutter, dash, quaver, throb, vibrate, burst, quell, (*adj*) break, crack, split.

anika spread; *synonyms* (*v*) scatter, reach, disperse, expand, extend, broadcast, circulate, diffuse, disseminate, increase, propagate, stretch, broaden, deploy, enlarge, dilate, distribute, open, range, smear, splay, display, run, (*n*) span, dissemination, expanse, expansion, feast, propagation, scattering; *antonym* (*adj*) concentrated.

anirIra shout; *synonyms* (*v*) cry, clamor, scream, bellow, bawl, exclaim, hollo, howl, shriek, hail, bark, holler, hoop, whoop, yelp, proclaim, chant, acclaim, squall, (*n*) call, roar, yell, cheer, halloo, outcry, screech, exclamation, wail, crow, vociferation; *antonym* (*v*) whisper.

arla speak; *synonyms* (*v*) express, converse, pronounce, articulate, deliver, say, utter, discourse, recite, talk, lecture, address, emit, mouth, state, vocalize, voice, mumble, prattle, declaim, read, reason, tongue, bespeak, handle, accost, chat, declare, exclaim, (*adj*) disclose.

atUra 1. crack; *synonyms* (*n*) break, fracture, cleft, fissure, chip, bump, blow, chap, cranny, gap, go, hit, shot, (*v*) chink, crevice, split, breach, burst, snap, clap, bang, check, cleave, rift, rupture, smash, whack, rend, boom, flaw; *antonyms* (*v*) repair, mend, **2**. split; *synonyms* (*v*) crack, cut, slit, divide, separate, divorce, division, fork, part, rive, sever, apportion, scatter, bisect, open, disunite, partition, share, splinter, disrupt, secede, (*adj*) cracked, disjointed, (*n*) rip, tear, cleavage, parting, chasm, hole, rent; *antonyms* (*v*) join, unite, merge.

B

baba father; *synonyms* (*n*) begetter, dad, sire, creator, abba, beginner, forefather, founder, padre, patriarch, author, parent, priest, clergyman, (*v*) beget, engender, create, generate, begin, breed, establish, found, get, initiate, make, mother, procreate, produce, start, (*adj*) doyen.

banga arrange; *synonyms* (*v*) adjust, appoint, dress, order, set, settle, pack, adapt, agree, classify, compose, decorate, do, engineer, fix, provide, put, reconcile, straighten, display, align, design, dispose, distribute, file, form, group, manage, marshal, (*n*) array; *antonyms* (*v*) disturb, disarrange.

bata 1. request; *synonyms* (*n*) petition, bid, prayer, application, claim, entreaty, wish, invitation, asking, command, quest, requisition, inquiry, offer, (*v*) demand, ask, invite, order, pray, appeal, beg, call, desire, entreat, beseech, inquire, seek, need, query, implore, **2.** need; *synonyms* (*v*) lack, require, destitution, indigence, involve, exact, have, take, crave, necessitate, (*n*) want, deficiency, must, necessity, deprivation, requirement, absence, beggary, distress, exigency, motive, hardship, dearth, essential, impoverishment, obligation, pauperism, penury, poverty, privation; *antonym* (*n*) wealth.

batabata flutter; *synonyms* (*n*) bustle, flap, wave, waver, agitation, excitement, quiver, thrill, tremble, flapping, pant, dither, (*v*) flicker, beat, flit, flitter, palpitate, fly, fluctuate, hover, shake, stir, fleet, vacillate, blow, falter, (*adj*) flurry, fluster, fidget, fuss.

bembe maize; *synonyms* (*n*) corn, cereal, gamboge, lemon, grain, buckwheat, clavus, millet, oats, rice, rye, stinker, wheat.

bUrUrI 1. district; *synonyms* (*n*) area, quarter, region, community, neighborhood, territory, circuit, county, field, jurisdiction, province, section, domain, constituency, country, ground, hemisphere, locality, municipality, part, place, realm, sector, sphere, state, tract, vicinity, ward, (*adj*) local, (*v*) zone, **2.** country; *synonyms* (*n*) nation, home, land, commonwealth, kingdom, soil, district, nationality, terrain, arena, (*adj*) rural, rustic, public, provincial, arable, pastoral; *antonyms* (*n*) city, (*adj*) urban, **3.** province; *synonyms* (*n*) colony, duty, function, line, dominion, division, range, office, responsibility, possession, (*v*) department.

C

cagUra 1. set up; *synonyms* (*v*) build, erect, raise, establish, found, assemble, construct, institute, mount, rear, arrange, create, fix, frame, install, introduce, organize, pitch, prepare, entrap, devise, elevate, launch, order, set, ready, organise, constitute, base, develop; *antonym* (*v*) disband, **2.** appoint; *synonyms* (*v*) assign, nominate, accredit, delegate, designate, prescribe, choose, commission, depute, destine, elect, make, ordain, hire, allot, attach, allocate, call, charge, command, consign, detail, employ, equip, furnish, outfit, place, point, select, (*n*) name.

cambia slander; *synonyms* (*n*) insult, scandal, aspersion, defamation, obloquy, disparagement, backbiting, calumny, denigration, disgrace, detraction, vilification, (*v*) libel, defame, calumniate, denigrate, disparage, backbite, blacken, belie, besmirch, reproach, smear, sully, tarnish, traduce, vilify, (*adj*) abuse, asperse, malign; *antonym* (*v*) praise.

cecenia pinch; *synonyms* (*n*) arrest, crisis, emergency, squeeze, twinge, exigency, modicum, dash, bit,

catch, collar, difficulty, hint, mite, (*v*) nip, compress, lift, wring, bite, clip, constrict, filch, gripe, pilfer, steal, pass, skimp, distress, nick, rob.

cemUra boil; *synonyms* (*v*) seethe, bubble, churn, simmer, ferment, burn, effervesce, fume, heat, anger, gurgle, cook, foam, froth, roast, (*n*) abscess, blister, furuncle, pimple, boiling, bump, eruption, pustule, swelling, seed, (*adj*) sore, rave, fester, stew, ulcer; *antonym* (*v*) freeze.

cenjia change; *synonyms* (*n*) shift, alteration, barter, modification, variation, move, adjustment, alternation, amendment, commutation, conversion, development, difference, flux, (*v*) exchange, alter, adapt, alternate, cash, convert, switch, transpose, turn, twist, affect, adjust, amend, commute, correct, interchange; *antonyms* (*v*) stay, leave, idle, maintain.

cera walk; *synonyms* (*v*) ramble, course, hike, move, roam, travel, trek, go, promenade, track, foot, ambulate, ambulation, journey, tramp, traverse, amble, hoof, mosey, (*n*) step, gait, pace, path, saunter, stroll, excursion, pass, turn, trip, constitutional.

ciarwo be born; *synonyms* (*v*) originate, begin, start, emerge.

cimba dig; *synonyms* (*v*) jab, delve, prod, burrow, comprehend, excavate, investigate, probe, apprehend, compass, drudge, grasp, grind, hollow, push, rummage, scoop, thrust, shove, research, (*n*) poke, excavation, gibe, punch, stab, taunt, crack, nudge, barb, digging; *antonym* (*n*) compliment.

cimbUria 1. dig up; *synonyms* (*v*) dig, excavate, exhume, unearth, find, uncover; *antonym* (*v*) bury, **2.** dig out; *synonyms* (*v*) remove, rummage, scoop, hollow, apprehend, channel, compass, comprehend, deepen, delve, dislodge, furrow, hunt, mine, search, tunnel, undermine, burrow, develop, drudge, expand, extend, extract, fag, flush, grasp, grind, grub, jab, labor.

cina 1. roast; *synonyms* (*adj*) roasted, (*n*) ridicule, joint, knock, parody, (*v*) broil, burn, bake, grill, joke, heat, quiz, cook, fry, scorch, tease, banter, chaff, slam, boil, twit, criticize, inflame, rally, **2.** singe; *synonyms* (*v*) char, sear, parch, roast, scald, swinge, **3.** burn; *synonyms* (*v*) bite, glow, blaze, incinerate, sting, beam, cremate, flare, ignite, sunburn, seethe, smolder, cauterize, color, kindle, radiate, runnel, shine, smart, damage, swelter, (*n*) fire, burning, creek, stream, tan, (*adj*) flush, smoke, simmer; *antonym* (*v*) dawdle, **4.** heap up; *synonyms* (*v*) amass, accumulate, gather, pile, collect, compile, load.

cinda 1. overcome; *synonyms* (*v*) conquer, beat, crush, subdue, vanquish, defeat, master, overpower, hurdle, overwhelm, prevail, subjugate, surmount, demolish, affect, cross, exceed, outdo, overbear, overtake, overthrow, quell, repress, suppress, triumph, trounce, (*adj*) beaten, conquered, overwhelmed, prostrate; *antonyms* (*v*) fail, (*adj*) victorious, unimpressed, **2.** vanquish; *synonyms* (*v*) overcome, rout, thrash, drub, lick, overmaster, discomfit, whip, get, reduce, tame, confound, baffle, cheat, pound, surpass, thump; *antonym* (*v*) lose, **3.** win; *synonyms* (*v*) acquire, gain, attain, obtain, achieve, earn, secure, take, succeed, carry, procure, reach, score, hit, make, receive, profit, gather, capture, accomplish, extract, finish, derive, deserve, realize, reap, seize, (*n*) profits, conquest, success.

ciothe all; *synonyms* (*adv*) whole, purely, altogether, entirely, totally, wholly, apiece, completely, quite, utterly, (*adj*) universal, each, every, gross, complete, alone, entire, outright, (*n*) aggregate, entirety, everything, sum, total, (*det*) any; *antonyms* (*pron*) none, (*det*) some.

ciUma bead; *synonyms* (*n*) drop, astragal, beading, pearl, dot, beadwork, bubble, drip, droplet, globule, (*v*) beautify, adorn.

coka 1. go back; *synonyms* (*v*) retreat, return, recede, recur, regress, revert, withdraw, revisit, turn, convalesce, deliver, devolve, fall, find, generate, give, recover, remember, reverse, abandon, betray, change, degenerate, desert, ebb, forsake, pass, recall, reclaim, recoup, **2.** return; *synonyms* (*n*) yield, pay, recompense, refund, restitution, proceeds, income, revenue, profit, relapse, comeback, compensation, issue, payment, produce, reappearance, recession, recurrence, redress, (*v*) reimburse, render, repay, restoration, restore, retort, answer, reinstate, reply, requite, repayment; *antonyms* (*n*) departure, abolition, confiscation, recovery, (*v*) keep.

cokanIriria pack; *synonyms* (*n*) bundle, mob, bevy, bunch, company, herd, batch, backpack, box, gang, horde, package, knapsack, cluster, bag, flock, group, knot, lot, multitude, (*v*) crowd, compress, heap, cram, fill, jam, load, carry, compact, crush; *antonym* (*v*) unpack.

cokia ciuria answer; *synonyms* (*n*) reply, respond, retort, return, solution, defense, echo, reaction, response, riposte, key, explanation, rejoinder, (*v*) counter, resolve, serve, acknowledge, agree, correspond, do, suffice, suit, refute, accord, fill, fit, fulfill, meet, react, (*adj*) pay; *antonyms* (*v*) question, ask.

conoka shame; *synonyms* (*n*) reproach, disgrace, discredit, humiliation, chagrin, insult, modesty, pity, scandal, contempt, degradation, embarrassment, humble, ignominy, infamy, mortification, opprobrium, odium, guilt, disrepute, (*v*) dishonor, degrade, humiliate, abash, debase, confuse, embarrass, discountenance, attaint, dishonour; *antonym* (*v*) honor.

cuba bottle; *synonyms* (*n*) container, flask, jug, jar, pot, carboy, gourd, (*v*) preserve, can.

cUcU grandmother; *synonyms* (*n*) gran, grandma, granny, crone, grandam, grannie, mother, dam, grandmamma, beldame, mamma, materfamilias, matriarch.

cuma steel; *synonyms* (*n*) harden, blade, brand, brace, foil, fortify, sword, invigorate, strengthen, (*adj*) iron, adamant, (*v*) nerve, temper, gird.

cunga 1. filter; *synonyms* (*n*) strainer, (*v*) percolate, sieve, drip, leak, filtrate, ooze, purify, refine, screen, strain, dribble, drop, clean, permeate, riddle, sift, trickle, besom, broom; *antonym* (*v*) contaminate, **2.** strain; *synonyms* (*n*) stress, breed, effort, stretch, exertion, race, reach, song, stock, type, air, attempt, crick, force, form, labor, line, melody, pressure, sprain, (*v*) filter, tax, endeavor, exert, extend, pull, try, burden, sort, strive; *antonym* (*v*) relax.

E

ega makIria 1. fine; *synonyms* (*adj*) delicate, agreeable, dainty, brave, capital, elegant, excellent, nice, thin, delightful, acute, admirable, alright, beautiful, choice, exquisite, glorious, pleasant, polite, stunning, superior, terrific, well, exact, bright, (*n*) penalty, amercement, (*v*) punish, mulct, clarify; *antonyms* (*adj*) poor, thick, coarse, substantial, unsatisfactory, wide, **2.** excellent; *synonyms* (*adj*) estimable, distinctive, brilliant, fantastic, fine, good, great, magnificent, marvelous, outstanding, perfect, splendid, superb, tremendous, wonderful, celebrated, commendable, famous, golden, crack, classic, better, complete, exceptional, exemplary, fabulous, grand, ideal, incomparable, (*n*) worthy; *antonyms* (*adj*) inferior, abysmal, awful, mediocre.

eheria send away; *synonyms* (*v*) dismiss, sack, eject, fire, expel, can, drop, evict.

F

fUmba dead person; *synonyms* (*n*) deceased, decedent, departed, fatality.

G

gacIra path; *synonyms* (*n*) course, direction, way, highway, line, orbit, track, lane, means, alley, avenue, corridor, itinerary, route, trace, walk, manner, aisle, approach, range, access, footstep, boulevard, conduit, passageway, road, run, street, thoroughfare, (v) passage.

gacUmbiri 1. utmost; *synonyms* (*adj*) extreme, farthest, last, supreme, uttermost, furthest, highest, greatest, ultimate, farthermost, most, outermost, paramount, top, final, terminal, chief, peak, main, (*n*) maximum, best, furthermost, limit, **2**. highest point; *synonyms* (*n*) pinnacle, zenith, ceiling, acme, apex, apogee, summit; *antonym* (*n*) base.

gagata ferment; *synonyms* (*n*) agitation, excitement, barm, tumult, unrest, disturbance, confusion, fermentation, fermenting, fume, restlessness, stir, turmoil, upheaval, warmth, yeast, zymosis, (*v*) effervesce, stew, turn, brew, fester, foam, agitate, ruffle, seethe, sour, work, (*adj*) pother, leaven.

garUra change; *synonyms* (*n*) shift, alteration, barter, modification, variation, move, adjustment, alternation, amendment, commutation, conversion, development, difference, flux, (*v*) exchange, alter, adapt, alternate, cash, convert, switch, transpose, turn, twist, affect, adjust, amend, commute, correct, interchange; *antonyms* (*v*) stay, leave, idle, maintain.

gatagatI inside; *synonyms* (*adv*) indoors, inwardly, within, (*n*) interior, middle, center, stomach, bosom, contents, (*adj*) inner, internal, indoor, inland, inward, private, privileged; *antonyms* (*prep*) outside, (*n*) exterior, (*adj*) free.

gatarU dugout canoe; *synonyms* (*n*) canoe, dugout, bunker, caique, felucca, pirogue.

gathanda mboiro canine tooth; *synonyms* (*n*) canine, cuspid, dogtooth, eyetooth, canid.

gathuku parrot; *synonyms* (*n*) poll, popinjay, (*v*) echo, mimic, ape, cuckoo, imitator, jay, magpie.

gaturu squirrel; *synonyms* (*n*) accumulator, collector, saver, magpie, miser, (*adj*) antelope, courser, doe, eagle, gazelle, greyhound, hare, chickaree, ostrich, scorcher, (*v*) bank, cache, conserve, deposit, harvest, hide, hoard, reserve, save, secrete, stint, store.

gayania divide; *synonyms* (*v*) cut, distribute, part, dissociate, apportion, detach, disconnect, dismember, dispense, separate, share, split, deal, distinguish, carve, disjoint, allot, class, classify, cleave, disjoin, disunite, diverge, sever, calculate, assign, chop, disengage, (*n*) break, watershed; *antonyms* (*v*) unite, join.

gemia decorate; *synonyms* (*v*) beautify, deck, adorn, bedeck, dress, embellish, grace, apparel, bedight, arrange, array, emblazon, embroider, enrich, garnish, hang, ornament, trim, paint, clothe; *antonym* (*v*) strip.

geria try; *synonyms* (*v*) attempt, test, struggle, prove, strive, assay, examine, experiment, judge, sample, strain, probe, seek, taste, adjudicate, aim, hear, render, undertake, afflict, demonstrate, (*n*) endeavor, essay, chance, effort, shot, go, trial, crack, endeavour.

getha 1. gather; *synonyms* (*v*) deduce, convene, accumulate, amass, assemble, collect, compile, congregate, flock, garner, meet, tuck, earn, rally, reap, derive, converge, extract, acquire, aggregate, cluster, conclude, crease, cull, gain, glean, group, harvest, infer, (*n*) fold; *antonyms* (*v*) disperse, scatter, **2**. reap; *synonyms* (*v*) get, cut, gather, obtain, receive, crop, draw, pick, pluck, attain, achieve, make, win, secure, (*adj*) mow, clip, prune, lop, shear, dock.

gicagi village; *synonyms* (*n*) hamlet, city, community, neighborhood, settlement, kraal, (*adv*) town.

gicango 1. brass wire, **2**. copper; *synonyms* (*n*) bronze, bull, cop, fuzz, gold, pig, cent, coin, ingot, nugget, cuprum, brown, copperplate, auburn, blur, bruiser, bullshit, buncombe, bunk, bunkum, change, detective, penny, red, silver, crap, dogshit, grunter, guff, hair, **3**. brass; *synonyms* (*n*) boldness, face, cheek, nerve, administration, arrogance, insolence, effrontery, impertinence, executive, management, (*v*) audacity, assurance, front, hardihood, impudence.

gIciko spoon; *synonyms* (*n*) ladle, spoonful, shovel, trowel, (*v*) scoop, smooch, dip, snog.

giciri shin; *synonyms* (*n*) shinbone, tibia, (*v*) clamber, scramble, shinny, abrade, bark, beat, fight, jumble, pare, peel, scrape, skin, sputter, struggle, shinney, splutter, stub.

gIIko 1. tobacco pipe; *synonyms* (*n*) pipe, tube, pipage, pipework, piping, **2**. spitting cobra.

gIko 1. rubbish; *synonyms* (*n*) refuse, garbage, litter, nonsense, trash, junk, offal, debris, drivel, hogwash, trumpery, waste, dirt, falderal, absurdity, folderol, rubble, balderdash, bull, bunk, codswallop, rot, tripe, twaddle, wreckage, applesauce, (*adj*) bosh; *antonym* (*n*) sense, **2**. act; *synonyms* (*n*) accomplishment, action, move, play, statute, decree, do, feat, law, performance, activity, edict, fact, (*v*) achievement, behave, deed, go, perform, acquit, enact, feign, operate, pretend, work, commit, conduct, fake, function, impersonate, make; *antonym* (*v*) refrain, **3**. garbage; *synonyms* (*n*) filth, hooey, rubbish, scrap, scraps, **4**. dirt; *synonyms* (*n*) soil, dust, grime, crap, ground, mire, scandal, contamination, smudge, dirtiness, foulness, impurity, land, muck, pollution, sludge, smut, squalor, stain, uncleanness, **5**. filth; *synonyms* (*n*) blot, filthiness, nastiness; *antonym* (*n*) cleanness.

gIkombe 1. mug; *synonyms* (*n*) countenance, pot, jug, chump, cup, face, kisser, sucker, tankard, victim, fool, mugful, phiz, physiognomy, pitcher, visage, bucket, photograph, (*v*) rob, grimace, attack, steal, **2**. pot; *synonyms* (*n*) caldron, boiler, can, belly, cannabis, commode, container, flowerpot, grass, heap, pan, pile, pool, urn, kitty, pickle, basin, bowl, ganja, hemp, jar, marihuana, mess, (v) bottle, cure, plant, (adj) deal, marijuana, volume, hashish.

gIkonde skin; *synonyms* (n) peel, hide, coating, fur, hull, rind, shell, crust, integument, pelt, case, coat, covering, cutis, fell, film, fleece, tegument, exterior, outside, envelope, (v) pare, bark, scrape, excoriate, flay, abrade, strip, chafe, remove.

gIkundi 1. pack; *synonyms* (n) bundle, mob, bevy, bunch, company, herd, batch, backpack, box, gang, horde, package, knapsack, cluster, bag, flock, group, knot, lot, multitude, (v) crowd, compress, heap, cram, fill, jam, load, carry, compact, crush; *antonym* (v) unpack, **2.** group; *synonyms* (n) brigade, collection, association, clump, gathering, lump, muster, assembly, assortment, category, circle, clique, community, congregation, division, ensemble, faction, line, mass, (v) assemblage, class, rank, sort, arrange, assemble, classify, collect, congregate, gather, order, **3.** flock; *synonyms* (n) band, covey, pack, troop, cloud, army, drove, pile, shoal, throng, rabble, legion, brood, host, plenty, raft, school, slew, spate, stack, wad, (v) flood, huddle, surge, meet, constellate, (adj) swarm, peck.

gIkunIko 1. cork; *synonyms* (n) bung, stopper, phellem, bob, bobber, bobfloat, (v) plug, cap, stop, close, (adj) cobweb, **2.** stopper; *synonyms* (n) stopple, top, closure, gate, (v) block, clog, obstruct.

gIkuU death; *synonyms* (n) demise, end, expiration, close, exit, cessation, decease, departure, dissolution, doom, dying, fate, loss, mortality, passing, conclusion, bereavement, extermination, fall, destruction, ending, finish, last, murder, (adj) quietus; *antonyms* (n) birth, existence, delivery.

girIka mourning; *synonyms* (n) grief, lament, lamentation, bereavement, gloom, sorrowfulness, sadness, sorrow, (v) lamenting, (adj) grieving.

girIrIria avoid; *synonyms* (v) shun, avert, parry, escape, evade, abstain, annul, circumvent, duck, elude, forbear, fudge, ignore, prevent, shirk, fly, beware, balk, debar, flee, help, invalidate, nullify, obviate, quash, refrain, void, decline, stop, (adj) eschew; *antonyms* (v) confront, associate, face, tackle; **girIrIria rUhuho** break wind.

girIrIria rUhuho break wind; *synonym* (v) fart.

gItara 1. nest; *synonyms* (n) den, lair, hole, burrow, home, herd, (v) nestle, (adj) brood, hive, litter, **2.** hole; *synonyms* (n) cavity, aperture, crack, pocket, breach, break, cave, corner, depression, fix, hollow, pit, vent, cavern, cranny, cell, crevice, excavation, jam, leak, opening, outlet, slit, tear, eye, nook, exit, crater, defect, (adj) gap.

gIthaka 1. thicket; *synonyms* (n) copse, brake, brush, coppice, grove, brushwood, bush, cluster, bunch, shrubbery, **2.** land; *synonyms* (n) ground, country, soil, field, kingdom, domain, estate, nation, realm, state, empire, commonwealth, demesne, property, dirt, grounds, area, (v) disembark, debark, alight,

get, drop, arrive, bring, down, perch, secure, acquire, impose, capture; *antonym* (adj) aquatic, **3.** bush; *synonyms* (n) shrub, bushing, wild, chaparral, hedge, jungle, plant, scrub, wilderness.

gIthima well; *synonyms* (adv) right, easily, thoroughly, considerably, fully, good, correctly, amply, intimately, nicely, properly, substantially, suitably, very, (adj) healthy, fit, shaft, sound, robust, hale, happy, hearty, whole, (n) fountain, spring, pit, hollow, fountainhead, (v) gush, issue; *antonyms* (adv) ill, badly, poorly, (adj) sick, unwell, dying, nauseous.

gIthimi 1. measure; *synonyms* (n) amount, criterion, extent, beat, benchmark, degree, estimate, measurement, meter, quantity, act, allotment, action, bill, dose, magnitude, pace, portion, proceeding, rate, scale, time, (v) grade, appraise, assess, evaluate, fathom, gauge, value, (adj) mete, **2.** size; *synonyms* (n) measure, bulk, capacity, dimension, dimensions, largeness, glue, breadth, mass, sizing, proportion, content, bigness, compass, enormity, fatness, format, greatness, length, number, paste, stature, cement, span, extension, area, body, bulkiness, (v) range, (adj) gum; *antonym* (n) slenderness.

gIthUri chest; *synonyms* (n) bosom, bust, box, bureau, case, casket, dresser, chamber, crate, thorax, treasury, trunk.

gIthUru chest; *synonyms* (n) bosom, bust, box, bureau, case, casket, dresser, chamber, crate, thorax, treasury, trunk.

gonyaria twist; *synonyms* (n) twine, wind, spin, twirl, entwine, braid, kink, loop, strain, tangle, convolution, crook, (v) turn, bend, distort, curl, coil, contort, deform, curve, pervert, wrench, pull, roll, sprain, bias, entangle, intertwine, convolute, garble; *antonyms* (v) straighten, untwist.

gua fall; *synonyms* (v) decline, dip, decrease, descend, dive, rain, diminish, dwindle, sink, alight, come, crash, fade, fail, light, lower, reduce, (n) drop, descent, downfall, plunge, pitch, cascade, collapse, cut, decay, declivity, deterioration, diminution, relapse; *antonyms* (v) rise, increase, ascend, climb, triumph, win, (n) ascent.

gUcama taste; *synonyms* (n) bit, flavor, liking, morsel, penchant, appetite, drink, drop, fondness, gusto, mouthful, predilection, preference, refinement, style, bite, discrimination, judgment, elegance, sapidity, sense, palate, (v) relish, savor, sample, smack, discernment, touch, try, gust; *antonyms* (n) dislike, tastelessness.

gucaria look for; *synonyms* (v) expect, hunt, anticipate, await, search, explore, rummage, seek.

gUcenjia 1. alter; *synonyms* (v) adapt, change, move, adjust, affect, amend, castrate, convert, correct, shift, transform, turn, vary, alternate, distort, diversify, edit, emasculate, exchange, fluctuate, invert, neuter, reverse, revise, translate, twist, deform, make, emend, reorganize; *antonym* (*v*) maintain, **2.** change; *synonyms* (*n*) alteration, barter, modification, variation, adjustment, alternation, amendment, commutation, conversion, development, difference, flux, upheaval, diversification, fluctuation, movement, mutation, (*v*) alter, cash, switch, transpose, commute, interchange, modify, replace, substitute, swap, transfer, dress, influence; *antonyms* (*v*) stay, leave, idle.

gucia 1. drag; *synonyms* (*v*) attract, haul, draw, puff, trail, cart, hale, heave, lug, tow, delay, shamble, delineate, dredge, force, inhale, lag, rake, shuffle, sweep, train, (*n*) pull, bother, bore, hindrance, inhalation, friction, clog, pressure, track; *antonym* (*v*) push, **2.** pull up; *synonyms* (*v*) stop, uproot, halt, raise, hike, hold; *antonym* (*v*) plant, **3.** pull out; *synonyms* (*v*) leave, extract, pluck, extend, remove, withdraw, abandon, depart, separate, break, retire, stretch, **4.** pull; *synonyms* (*v*) drag, draught, jerk, tug, pick, make, lure, strain, get, appeal, arrest, commit, tear, yank, charm, drive, fetch, interest, (*n*) wrench, attraction, effort, twist, influence, control, allure, tension, exertion, fascination, magnetism, proof; *antonym* (*v*) repel.

gucuna lick; *synonyms* (*v*) lap, clobber, bat, beat, drub, thrash, defeat, bang, trim, overcome, touch, trounce, wallop, whip, answer, resolve, rout, solve, (*n*) biff, jab, speed, dash, blow, punch.

gucunga sift; *synonyms* (*v*) screen, filter, investigate, analyze, examine, riddle, sieve, sprinkle, bolt, separate, sort, strain, probe, scatter, explore, inquire, discriminate, dust, select, try, brush, comb, debate, (*n*) scrutinize, canvass, search, anatomize, dissect, parse, resolve.

guIma hunt; *synonyms* (*n*) search, pursuit, quest, hunting, (*v*) chase, course, follow, hound, forage, rummage, prey, dog, persecute, pursue, seek, stalk, trace, track, trail, comb, dig, explore, look, run, scour, scrounge.

gUithia drop; *synonyms* (*v*) fall, decrease, deposit, dribble, droop, abandon, cast, dip, discard, dismiss, drip, ebb, jump, shed, sink, decay, die, cancel, crash, descend, deteriorate, diminish, (*n*) decline, collapse, spot, bead, cut, dash, descent, distill; *antonyms* (*v*) rise, increase, lift, (*n*) growth.

guka grandfather; *synonyms* (*n*) gramps, grandad, granddad, grandpa, grandpapa, grandsire, granddaddy, patriarch.

gukinya arrive; *synonyms* (*v*) come, mature, attain, fall, land, reach, succeed, show, derive, emerge, enter, get, happen, issue, prosper, disembark, (*n*) appear; *antonyms* (*v*) leave, depart, go.

gukiririra suffer; *synonyms* (*v*) bear, encounter, abide, accept, brook, endure, experience, have, stand, undergo, permit, receive, smart, sustain,

tolerate, pay, bide, feel, get, let, lose, meet, stomach, take, carry, grieve, languish, catch, (*adj*) allow, ail.

gUkomba borrow; *synonyms* (*v*) adopt, appropriate, assume, take, accept, acquire, plagiarize, cadge, obtain, sponge, usurp, charter, copy, imitate, annex, beg, steal, absorb, arrogate, bear, cheat, creance, desume, infringe, pilfer, simulate, bite, bum, capture, (*n*) pledge; *antonym* (*v*) lend.

gUkUra grow up; *synonyms* (*v*) develop, mature, age, mellow.

gukuria bring up; *synonyms* (*v*) breed, nurture, raise, rear, mention, advance, develop, educate, foster, propose, vomit, advert, allude, arouse, boot, cite, elevate, lift, refer.

guoko 1. hand; *synonyms* (*n*) deal, aid, applause, employee, paw, worker, support, assist, assistance, handwriting, help, indicator, mitt, needle, (*v*) deliver, give, pass, commit, bestow, afford, communicate, reach, grant, provide, devolve, line, gift, supply, feed, distribute, **2.** arm; *synonyms* (*n*) branch, wing, bay, department, division, limb, might, offshoot, power, section, sleeve, weapon, endow, member, (*v*) equip, furnish, outfit; *antonym* (*v*) disarm.

guoya fear; *synonyms* (*n*) apprehension, awe, alarm, dismay, doubt, anguish, care, consternation, foreboding, fright, trepidation, worry, anxiety, disquiet, fearfulness, intimidation, panic, terror, trouble, diffidence, funk, misgiving, phobia, respect, (*v*) dread, concern, reverence, affright, apprehend, revere; *antonyms* (*n*) bravery, confidence, fearlessness, reassurance.

gurya bend; *synonyms* (*n*) bow, arch, arc, elbow, twist, angle, curvature, bending, buckle, flexure, kink, round, (*v*) curve, turn, crouch, stoop, crook, curl, flex, deflect, fold, loop, swerve, wind, contort, cower, deform, distort, hunch, incline; *antonyms* (*v*) straighten, square.

gutaha maI draw; *synonyms* (*v*) attract, drag, delineate, pull, depict, derive, describe, design, tie, bring, charm, haul, lure, puff, get, make, outline, pluck, carry, deduce, elongate, bait, doodle, absorb, cart, cast, (*n*) allure, attraction, draft, appeal; *antonyms* (*v*) push, repel.

gutenderUka slip; *synonyms* (*n*) lapse, fault, mistake, cutting, error, escape, oversight, scion, trip, ticket, band, dip, gaffe, strip, note, petticoat, shred, (*v*) fall, slide, drop, glide, skid, sag, shift, sneak, stumble, tumble, decline, (*adj*) blunder, omission; *antonym* (*v*) improve.

gUtha rUhi slap; *synonyms* (*n*) smack, cuff, blow, hit, whack, spank, plump, rap, slam, stroke, swipe, tap, sock, touch, (*v*) clap, knock, beat, buffet, strike, box, crack, bump, pat, punch, thump, bash, (*adv*) bang, directly, right, bolt.

gUthaya lazy; *synonyms* (*adj*) indolent, idle, inert, drowsy, inactive, shiftless, dull, faineant, remiss, slothful, slow, sluggish, leisurely, sluggard, tardy, apathetic, careless, easygoing, languid, listless, negligent, otiose, slack, sedentary, (*n*) heavy, sleepy; *antonyms* (*adj*) energetic, diligent, active.

guthIIna travel; *synonyms* (*n*) journey, pass, stroke, passage, tour, voyage, locomotion, traffic, trip, jaunt, (*v*) go, run, proceed, move, roam, ride, cruise, ramble, sail, drive, range, track, advance, progress, walk, wander, meander, rove, circulate, (*adj*) course.

guthika stop up; *synonyms* (*v*) clog, block, plug, seal, close, obstruct, secure.

gUthira 1. cease; *synonyms* (*v*) end, break, quit, stop, terminate, abstain, close, conclude, discontinue, drop, desist, expire, halt, lapse, leave, pause, block, abandon, cut, die, perish, refrain, stay, stint, suspend, disappear, (*n*) finish, termination, cessation, (*adj*) abate; *antonyms* (*v*) continue, begin, **2.** finish; *synonyms* (*v*) complete, achieve, execute, accomplish, cease, determine, consume, do, culminate, deplete, exhaust, go, result, dispatch, drain, fulfill, (*n*) consummate, conclusion, death, ending, finale, glaze, accomplishment, coating, completion, last, closing, coat, face, finis; *antonyms* (*v*) start, (*n*) beginning.

gUthiUrUrUka surround; *synonyms* (*v*) encircle, circle, gird, border, compass, inclose, ring, round, skirt, beset, besiege, circumvent, embrace, enclose, envelop, environ, circumscribe, entwine, bound, beleaguer, blockade, edge, encompass, enfold, fence, invest, smother, (*n*) environment, environs, wreathe.

gUtigana 1. divorce; *synonyms* (*n*) separation, divorcement, rupture, (*v*) detach, dissociate, disunite, separate, divide, isolate, disjoin, disjoint, disassociate, part, sever, split, break; *antonyms* (*n*) marriage, wedding, **2.** separate; *synonyms* (*adj*) detached, individual, particular, single, disjoined, distinct, diverse, free, isolated, abstract, other, apart, (*v*) divorce, insulate, scatter, cut, disconnect, discrete, discriminate, disperse, distinguish, demarcate, differentiate, disengage, dissolve, leave, remove, segregate, decompose, secede; *antonyms* (*adj*) connected, joined, simultaneous, (*v*) unite, merge, mix, combine, fuse, join, link, associate.

gUtigwo remain; *synonyms* (*v*) endure, bide, continue, linger, stay, keep, last, persist, live, hold, be, dwell, persevere, stand, delay, exist, reside, rest, stick, attend, lie, detain, hang, inhabit, retain, subsist, survive, tarry, prevail, (*n*) abide; *antonym* (*v*) leave.

gUtindika push; *synonyms* (*n*) press, thrust, jolt, poke, elbow, energy, jerk, (*v*) drive, impel, crowd, force, jab, jostle, nudge, prod, jam, rush, boost, fight, incite, jog, labor, plug, pressure, promote, shove, campaign, crusade, strain, work; *antonyms* (*v*) pull, drag, haul.

gUtinia slash; *synonyms* (*n*) cut, gash, rip, slice, split, cleft, diagonal, scratch, blaze, (*v*) reduce, hack, clip,

hew, tear, wound, fell, chop, flog, lash, slit, whip, pare, strike, abridge, decrease, crop, drop, slam, carve, curtail.

gUtU ear; *synonyms* (*n*) auricle, handle, hearing, lug, spike, capitulum, heed, earing, notice, crown, pinna, appreciation, discrimination, favor, mark, observance, observation, perception, pinnule, scallop, sensitivity, taste, treetop, (*v*) cultivate.

gutuamo sink; *synonyms* (*n*) sag, basin, (*v*) decline, dip, droop, fall, set, descend, drop, fell, bury, collapse, decay, flag, founder, lower, settle, subside, ebb, languish, abate, decrease, die, plunge, fade, disappear, degenerate, deteriorate, (*adj*) immerse, bog; *antonyms* (*v*) rise, float.

gutukania 1. put together; *synonyms* (*v*) erect, assemble, build, combine, construct, join, prepare, create, fabricate, form, organize, frame, make, produce, arrange, compose, weave, compile, incorporate, mix, raise, configure, connect, edify, manufacture, piece, place, (*adv*) collectively, conjointly, jointly, **2.** compose; *synonyms* (*v*) allay, constitute, tranquilize, write, adjust, compound, pen, settle, list, comprise, design, draft, draw, formulate, indite, invent, set, outline, collect, alleviate, coin, control, cool, edit, (*adj*) assuage, appease, lull, pacify, soothe, (*n*) calm.

gutUma spring; *synonyms* (*n*) jump, leap, bound, fountain, skip, source, dance, rise, jet, cause, font, fount, ramp, well, run, (*v*) hop, caper, bounce, dive, originate, recoil, proceed, arise, issue, prance, rebound, vault, pounce, stem, (*adj*) elastic.

gUtumia kanua close; *synonyms* (*adj*) near, adjacent, nearby, accurate, tight, approximate, narrow, brief, airless, complete, hot, immediate, intimate, parsimonious, (*v*) compact, stop, conclude, bar, block, fold, seal, (*adv*) by, about, nigh, (*n*) end, finish, conclusion, expiration, ending, finale; *antonyms* (*adj*) distant, airy, fresh, loose, far, (*v*) open, start.

gutwarana 1. harmonise; *synonyms* (*v*) accord, agree, harmonize, reconcile, accommodate, concur, correspond, chord, conciliate, consort, **2.** match; *synonyms* (*n*) equal, competition, couple, duplicate, peer, bout, contest, game, tally, associate, catch, (*v*) mate, meet, parallel, harmonise, balance, fellow, fit, pair, coincide, equalize, equate, jibe, marry, rival, suit, twin, compare, adapt, check; *antonyms* (*v*) clash, contradict.

gUtwekia melt; *synonyms* (*v*) fuse, dissolve, deliquesce, run, thaw, vanish, coalesce, combine, fade, heat, meld, mellow, relent, soften, flow, touch, blend, disappear, flux, resolve, subdue, unfreeze, commingle, conflate, (*n*) warming, melting, thawing, (*adj*) liquefy, go, course; *antonyms* (*v*) freeze, cool, solidify.

gwatania splice; *synonyms* (*n*) joint, junction, splicing, (*v*) link, conjoin, join, marry, wed, inosculate, twine, anastomose, calk, careen, caulk, dovetail, graft, (*adj*) tie, braid, lace.

gwathimUra sneeze; *synonyms* (*v*) arrest, (*n*) sneezing, sternutation.

gweta pronounce; *synonyms* (*v*) enunciate, articulate, affirm, declare, say, assert, deliver, express, utter, announce, decree, judge, proclaim, rule, speak, vocalize, pass, adjudicate, enounce, state, voice, prolate, aver, comment, (*n*) allege, give, maintain, adjudge, contend, (*adj*) discharge.

gwIciria 1. imagine; *synonyms* (*v*) think, believe, conjecture, assume, conceive, daydream, fancy, guess, consider, devise, envision, fantasize, see, visualize, calculate, image, divine, gather, apprehend, deduce, envisage, expect, hypothesize, ideate, picture, pretend, project, reckon, (*conj*) suppose, (*n*) dream, **2.** think; *synonyms* (*v*) estimate, hold, imagine, muse, ponder, reflect, regard, cogitate, contemplate, deliberate, meditate, reason, study, suspect, deem, esteem, feel, intend, recollect, figure, repute, cerebrate, judge, mean, opine, presume, recall, remember, remind, understand; *antonym* (*v*) forget.

gwItIa kwIgana 1. boast; *synonyms* (*v*) bluster, vaunt, blow, brag, crow, gasconade, pride, rodomontade, exult, bounce, exaggerate, flourish, sport, swagger, swash, avaunt, crack, (*n*) arrogance, boasting, glory, jactitation, **2.** brag; *synonyms* (*v*) boast, (*n*) bragging, vapor, crowing, (*adj*) boss.

H

haha here; *synonyms* (*adv*) hither, in, about, arrived, available, indoors, inwards, (*n*) hair, (*adj*) present, there, near, nearby, (*pron*) her, their; *antonym* (*adv*) out.

haita 1. ascend; *synonyms* (*v*) rise, arise, mount, climb, scale, uprise, increase, appear, escalate, jump, lift, soar; *antonyms* (*v*) descend, drop, **2.** climb; *synonyms* (*v*) ascend, clamber, scramble, bestride, fly, (*n*) ascent, acclivity, advance, ascending, ascension, climbing, hike, mounting, raise, upgrade, ramble.

haka spread; *synonyms* (*v*) scatter, reach, disperse, expand, extend, broadcast, circulate, diffuse, disseminate, increase, propagate, stretch, broaden, deploy, enlarge, dilate, distribute, open, range, smear, splay, display, run, (*n*) span, dissemination, expanse, expansion, feast, propagation, scattering; *antonym* (*adj*) concentrated.

hakuhI near; *synonyms* (*prep*) about, by, around, (*adv*) close, almost, towards, approximately, nearly, beside, closely, most, (*adj*) adjoining, adjacent, contiguous, imminent, impending, narrow, coming, closer, handy, stingy, mean, miserly, cheeseparing, immediate, (*v*) familiar, approximate, approach, intimate, come; *antonym* (*adj*) distant.

hanana resemble; *synonyms* (*v*) imitate, seem, compare, correspond, agree, look, match, simulate, approximate, echo.

handa 1. sow; *synonyms* (*n*) pig, hog, swine, bitch, boar, hen, (*v*) scatter, disperse, broadcast, inseminate, seed, disseminate, plant, sough, farm, distribute, propagate, spread, **2.** plant; *synonyms* (*n*) manufactory, equipment, factory, herb, mill, bush, cheat, flora, works, (*v*) fix, place, embed, graft, set, constitute, establish, found, lay, bury, cultivate, appoint, nominate, engraft, imbed, implant, install, institute, afforest, ingraft, erect.

handu place; *synonyms* (*n*) position, domicile, office, order, spot, attitude, base, job, location, situation, circumstance, center, abode, berth, dwelling, (*v*) post, arrange, fix, lay, locate, rank, station, deposit, install, pitch, put, set, lie, commit, dispose; *antonym* (*v*) remove.

hanyUkia chase; *synonyms* (*n*) game, search, quest, following, (*v*) hunt, pursue, expel, follow, stalk, track, trail, chamfer, pursuit, race, seek, evict, course, dog, drive, furrow, oust, shadow, shoot, tag, tail, woo, (*adj*) emboss.

haraya far; *synonyms* (*adv*) wide, off, widely, well, astray, (*adj*) distant, aloof, faraway, remote, much, outlying, (*v*) considerably, abundantly; *antonyms* (*adv*) close, briefly, (*adj*) near.

haria there; *synonyms* (*adv*) here, thither, present, thereat, apparent, convenient, visible, around, manifest, obvious, within, (*adj*) adept, competent, expert, professional, reliable, skillful, trustworthy, unfailing, near, nearby.

hata 1. sweep; *synonyms* (*n*) compass, expanse, range, scope, field, stretch, area, room, expansion, slam, spread, turn, wave, (*v*) brush, rake, reach, sail, sway, shot, broom, clean, cross, drag, skim, span, swing, fly, scavenger, (*adj*) curve, comb, **2.** sweep up; *synonyms* (*v*) sweep, embrace, embroil, espouse, acquire, adopt, assume, borrow, bosom, cart, comprehend, conjoin, cover, dishevel, dramatise, dramatize, draw, dredge, encompass, entangle, follow, hale, haul, hug, knot, marry, mat, puff, ravel, scoop.

he 1. borrow; *synonyms* (*v*) adopt, appropriate, assume, take, accept, acquire, plagiarize, cadge, obtain, sponge, usurp, charter, copy, imitate, annex, beg, steal, absorb, arrogate, bear, cheat, creance, desume, infringe, pilfer, simulate, bite, bum, capture, (*n*) pledge; *antonym* (*v*) lend, **2.** lend; *synonyms* (*v*) loan, advance, give, grant, add, bestow, bring, contribute, impart, confer, provide; *antonym* (*v*) borrow.

heana give away; *synonyms* (*v*) disclose, give, betray, distribute, divulge, expose, reveal, bestow, dispense, present, abandon, blab, contribute, bewray, donate, discover, display, impart, tell, uncover, unveil, denounce, drop, expropriate, forego, leak.

heana rutha send away; *synonyms* (*v*) dismiss, sack, eject, fire, expel, can, drop, evict.

heho cold; *synonyms* (*adj*) chilly, frigid, aloof, callous, distant, icy, indifferent, apathetic, bleak, cool, dead, dull, freezing, frosty, hard, heartless, impassive, inhospitable, lukewarm, reserved, stale, standoffish, unemotional, unfeeling, unfriendly, unsympathetic, polar, austere, (*n*) chilliness, chill; *antonyms* (*adj*) warm, friendly, hot, burning, prepared, affectionate, loving, soporific, (*n*) heat, warmth.

hiha 1. press out; *synonyms* (*v*) express, extract, distill, extinguish, press, **2.** milk; *synonyms* (*v*) exploit, squeeze, drain, tap, anodyne, balm, bleed, (*adj*) albumen, chalk, glair, gluten, **3.** squeeze; *synonyms* (*v*) hug, compress, pinch, embrace, extort, cram, crush, force, jam, nip, pack, squash, compact, condense, constrict, oppress, contract, crowd, cuddle, mash, pressure, push, ram, reduce, wring, narrow, screw, clasp, (*n*) grip, hold; *antonym* (*v*) loosen.

hihia roast; *synonyms* (*adj*) roasted, (*n*) ridicule, joint, knock, parody, (*v*) broil, burn, bake, grill, joke, heat, quiz, cook, fry, scorch, tease, banter, chaff, slam, boil, twit, criticize, inflame, rally.

hIhihia roast; *synonyms* (*adj*) roasted, (*n*) ridicule, joint, knock, parody, (*v*) broil, burn, bake, grill, joke, heat, quiz, cook, fry, scorch, tease, banter, chaff, slam, boil, twit, criticize, inflame, rally.

hikania marry; *synonyms* (*v*) join, link, conjoin, splice, tie, unite, wive, couple, combine, merge, connect, unify, match, pair, adopt, embrace, (*n*) espouse, wed, (*adj*) indeed; *antonym* (*v*) divorce.

hinanana resemble; *synonyms* (*v*) imitate, seem, compare, correspond, agree, look, match, simulate, approximate, echo.

hindi grain; *synonyms* (*n*) corn, crumb, bit, berry, cereal, fragment, atom, character, grist, kernel, scrap, speck, buckwheat, cast, iota, dash, molecule, particle, surface, texture, vein, caryopsis, (*v*) granulate, tint, color, dye, enamel, furbish, (*adj*) seed, spirit.

hinga 1. power; *synonyms* (*n*) force, ability, potency, authority, control, energy, agency, domination, intensity, strength, effectiveness, effect, aptitude, capability, command, gift, jurisdiction, mightiness, rule, vigor, weight, mastery, function, efficiency, (*v*) influence, might, dominion, faculty, capacity, efficacy; *antonyms* (*n*) powerlessness, helplessness, weakness, **2.** strength; *synonyms* (*n*) power, firmness, endurance, stability, health, soundness, amount, brawn, forcefulness, forte, fortitude, lustiness, magnitude, muscle, solidity, stoutness, sturdiness, toughness, measure, momentum, durability, fierceness, hardness, permanence,

resistance, stamina, substance, validity, sinew, (*v*) main; *antonyms* (*n*) frailty, flaw, shortcoming.

hingwo stumble; *synonyms* (*v*) slip, fall, flounder, fumble, err, falter, hit, stammer, bumble, reel, totter, tumble, wobble, sin, hobble, founder, hesitate, (*n*) trip, lurch, misstep, stagger, error, failure, mistake, (*adj*) blunder, botch, fault, bungle, oversight, boggle.

hita 1. swear; *synonyms* (*v*) affirm, assert, assure, curse, declare, avow, depone, depose, pledge, attest, asseverate, insist, blaspheme, cuss, damn, guarantee, imprecate, insult, rely, vow, maintain, trust, warrant, bank, claim, hold, swan, (*n*) promise, aver, avouch, **2.** hunt; *synonyms* (*n*) search, pursuit, quest, hunting, (*v*) chase, course, follow, hound, forage, rummage, prey, dog, persecute, pursue, seek, stalk, trace, track, trail, comb, dig, explore, look, run, scour, scrounge.

hitha hide; *synonyms* (*v*) conceal, disguise, obscure, bury, cloak, mask, shelter, ambush, muffle, camouflage, dissemble, enshroud, envelop, shade, shield, shroud, withhold, wrap, becloud, (*n*) cover, fur, coat, fell, skin, veil, cloud, bark, fleece, pelt, (*adj*) darken; *antonyms* (*v*) reveal, show, expose, express.

hiti hyena; *synonyms* (*n*) hyaena, hyen, tiger.

hItUka 1. pass; *synonyms* (*v*) flow, deliver, give, happen, lead, move, offer, overtake, live, advance, die, elapse, exceed, extend, lapse, leave, proceed, surpass, make, approve, befall, authorize, clear, convey, decease, (*n*) fare, crack, cut, (*adj*) go, run; *antonym* (*v*) fail, **2.** surpass; *synonyms* (*v*) pass, beat, outdo, better, excel, outstrip, surmount, overcome, overrun, best, outgo, outshine, outweigh, overstep, top, break, overshadow, overreach, cap, outdistance, outmatch, transcend, transgress, circumvent, outrank, rival, spend, overhaul, outperform, hand.

hiUhia boil; *synonyms* (*v*) seethe, bubble, churn, simmer, ferment, burn, effervesce, fume, heat, anger, gurgle, cook, foam, froth, roast, (*n*) abscess, blister, furuncle, pimple, boiling, bump, eruption, pustule, swelling, seed, (*adj*) sore, rave, fester, stew, ulcer; *antonym* (*v*) freeze.

hona 1. escape; *synonyms* (*v*) elude, break, dodge, avoid, evade, run, bolt, circumvent, leave, duck, bilk, abscond, desert, elope, ooze, scape, bleed, bunk, disappear, neglect, (*n*) leak, avoidance, evasion, outlet, deliverance, egress, flight, leakage, shunning, efflux; *antonyms* (*v*) capture, return, **2.** recover; *synonyms* (*v*) reclaim, recuperate, regain, retrieve, convalesce, find, heal, mend, rally, restore, improve, obtain, recall, recoup, redeem, repair, rescue, salvage, save, ransom, compensate, rebuild, recompense, rehabilitate, replevy, cure, discover, get, recruit, reimburse; *antonyms* (*v*) deteriorate, lose, **3.** get well; *synonyms* (*v*) recover, cover, cross, master, overcome, subdue, surmount, track, traverse.

honoka 1. escape; *synonyms (v)* elude, break, dodge, avoid, evade, run, bolt, circumvent, leave, duck, bilk, abscond, desert, elope, ooze, scape, bleed, bunk, disappear, neglect, *(n)* leak, avoidance, evasion, outlet, deliverance, egress, flight, leakage, shunning, efflux; *antonyms (v)* capture, return, **2.** recover; *synonyms (v)* reclaim, recuperate, regain, retrieve, convalesce, find, heal, mend, rally, restore, improve, obtain, recall, recoup, redeem, repair, rescue, salvage, save, ransom, compensate, rebuild, recompense, rehabilitate, replevy, cure, discover, get, recruit, reimburse; *antonyms (v)* deteriorate, lose.

hora get well; *synonyms (v)* heal, recover, recuperate, convalesce, improve, cover, cross, mend, recoup, regain, master, overcome, rally, subdue, surmount, track, traverse; *antonym (v)* deteriorate.

hoya ask for; *synonyms (v)* ask, invite, request, bid, attract, bespeak, challenge, encourage, incite, quest, requisition, risk, bay, betoken, buy, collect, crave, implore, importune, indicate, involve, necessitate, obtain, plead, point, receive, signal, supplicate, tempt; *antonym (v)* grant.

hUgUrUru 1. coast; *synonyms (n)* bank, beach, seaside, shore, seashore, sand, seacoast, shoreline, *(v)* glide, slide, drift, cruise; *antonym (n)* interior, **2.** beach; *synonyms (n)* coast, foreshore, strand, coastline, land.

huho disembodied spirit; *synonyms (n)* spirit, feel, feeling, flavor, flavour, heart, intent, life, liveliness, look, purport, smell, sprightliness, tone.

huhuho wind; *synonyms (n)* air, gust, clue, gale, intimation, suggestion, breath, flatus, hint, jazz, lead, *(v)* coil, twist, curl, meander, turn, bend, curve, twine, blow, crook, entwine, roll, weave, spiral, enlace, loop, nose, scent, snake.

huma 1. breathing; *synonyms (n)* breath, *(adj)* animate, live, living, alive, **2.** breath; *synonyms (n)* spirit, wind, air, inspiration, puff, aspiration, breather, breeze, flash, flatus, gust, instant, jiffy, respite, trice, twinkling, whiff, intimation, suggestion, trace, *(adj)* whisper.

hUmba 1. pile up; *synonyms (v)* accumulate, amass, gather, collect, hoard, conglomerate, cumulate, assemble, compile, exaggerate, garner, load, magnify, pack, **2.** stack; *synonyms (n)* pile, accumulation, mound, rick, mass, bunch, bundle, hill, mountain, shock, collection, haystack, batch, chimney, sheaf, smokestack, wad, bulk, cluster, drift, clump, cumulus, flock, mint, peck, *(v)* heap, lot, store, jam, cock, **3.** clothe; *synonyms (v)* array, dress, apparel, cover, garb, clad, arrange, deck, invest, vest, wrap, adorn, fit, rig, bedeck, drape, furnish, garment, habilitate, indue, swathe, enclothe, *(n)* attire, habit; *antonym (v)* undress, **4.** heap; *synonyms (n)* stack, group, congeries, gathering, crowd, multitude, aggregation, assemblage, deal, plenty, pot, raft, sight, slew,

stockpile, throng, bus, jalopy, *(v)* aggregate, bank, fill, lavish, *(adj)* myriad.

humbIra cover; *synonyms (v)* coat, conceal, top, bury, cloak, veil, wrap, comprise, bind, cross, drape, enclose, encompass, enfold, envelop, *(n)* blind, blanket, screen, binding, camouflage, cap, covering, lid, mask, shield, spread, coating, canopy, case, concealment; *antonyms (v)* reveal, expose, uncover.

hUmUka 1. breathe; *synonyms (v)* blow, exhale, live, subsist, be, emit, exist, imply, rest, whisper, inspire, convey, heave, huff, puff, survive, utter, *(n)* respire, bespeak, argue, **2.** rest; *synonyms (n)* remnant, repose, balance, pause, recess, relaxation, residue, leisure, break, quiet, respite, halt, intermission, interval, *(v)* nap, remain, sleep, ease, lie, perch, abide, recline, relief, stay, dwell, lean, depend, breathe, *(adj)* remainder, remains; *antonym (v)* work.

hUna whistling; *synonyms (n)* whistle, pennywhistle.

hUngU kite; *synonyms (n)* parachute, airplane, epistle, former, letter, slip, *(v)* scram.

hunia satisfy; *synonyms (v)* please, content, fill, indulge, meet, persuade, sate, satiate, appease, answer, assuage, convince, delight, execute, fulfill, gratify, serve, perform, feed, assure, compensate, discharge, fulfil, match, requite, settle, comply, cover, *(adj)* suffice, do; *antonyms (v)* dissatisfy, disappoint, displease, intensify.

hUra 1. wash; *synonyms (v)* rinse, paint, bathe, clean, lave, moisten, mop, scour, scrub, color, tint, lap, gargle, dampen, launder, splash, wet, dye, swill, *(n)* soak, ablution, washing, swamp, bath, laundry, lotion, marsh, swash, tinge, coat; *antonym (v)* dirty, **2.** beat; *synonyms (v)* batter, flap, pulsate, throb, tick, trounce, whip, bat, baste, break, cheat, clobber, crush, exceed, flog, grind, hammer, outdo, overwhelm, pound, rout, smite, strike, *(n)* pulse, thump, knock, round, cadence, hit, rap; *antonym (v)* lose.

hurara fight; *synonyms (v)* combat, contest, quarrel, feud, argue, bicker, campaign, clash, contend, encounter, compete, affray, box, crusade, drive, defend, *(n)* battle, dispute, engagement, conflict, contention, squabble, struggle, action, competition, confrontation, row, scuffle, war, *(adj)* brawl; *antonyms (v)* agree, retreat, withdrawal.

huria rhinoceros; *synonyms (n)* rhino, hippopotamus, pachyderm, rhinocerote, tapirs.

hurUka rest; *synonyms (n)* remnant, repose, balance, pause, recess, relaxation, residue, leisure, break, quiet, respite, halt, intermission, interval, *(v)* nap, remain, sleep, ease, lie, perch, abide, recline, relief, stay, dwell, lean, depend, breathe, *(adj)* remainder, remains; *antonym (v)* work.

hurutIra 1. wave; *synonyms (n)* billow, gesture, motion, sign, surge, signal, breaker, vibration, nod, rash, tide, undulation, (*v*) brandish, flap, flutter, curl, flourish, swell, swing, undulate, beat, beckon, ripple, shake, sway, oscillate, roll, kink, fluctuate, gesticulate, **2.** fan; *synonyms* (*n*) admirer, buff, devotee, enthusiast, addict, adherent, afficionado, fiend, follower, advocate, disciple, fanatic, lover, supporter, archer, palmetto, (*v*) air, winnow, refresh, blow, stimulate, ventilate, bellows, blowpipe, cool; *antonym* (*n*) detractor.

hUta hunger; *synonyms* (*n*) desire, thirst, appetite, craving, wish, itch, eagerness, famine, longing, starvation, yen, greed, hankering, hungriness, malnutrition, passion, yearning, keenness, voracity, (*v*) crave, want, ache, long, lust, yearn, covet, famish, languish, starve, envy; *antonym* (*n*) moderation.

hUthIra use; *synonyms* (*n*) custom, practice, benefit, habit, application, function, avail, consumption, enjoyment, help, purpose, (*v*) exercise, employ, employment, expend, profit, advantage, exploit, occupy, operate, spend, exert, need, enjoy, apply, take, treat, utilize, (*adj*) usage, service; *antonym* (*v*) conserve.

huuha blow up; *synonyms* (*adj*) detonate, explosion, (*v*) expand, explode, amplify, enlarge, inflate, magnify, puff, blast, burst, distend, rage, aggrandize, balloon, billow, erupt, pad, swell, bristle, develop, reprimand, seethe, (*n*) enlargement, anger; *antonym* (*v*) deflate.

huura 1. wipe; *synonyms* (*v*) rub, clean, mop, towel, brush, scour, scrub, clear, dry, wash, cover, (*n*) fling, flout, gibe, gleek, hiss, hoot, jeer, quip, scoff, sneer, taunt, (*adj*) sponge, flush, full, mundify, rinse, swab, **2.** grace; *synonyms* (*n*) elegance, favor, clemency, beauty, benediction, blessing, charm, benefit, forgiveness, pity, charity, comeliness, goodwill, mercy, (*v*) bedeck, adorn, deck, garnish, beautify, decorate, embellish, dress, embroider, enrich, dignify, bedight, ornament, (*adj*) goodness, beneficence, kindness, **3.** scrape; *synonyms* (*v*) scratch, graze, pare, rake, grate, mark, abrade, chafe, grind, claw, engrave, file, fray, rasp, skin, squeak, dent, skimp, grave, scoop, (*n*) score, abrasion, predicament, difficulty, quagmire, dilemma, cut, fix, plight, scraping.

I

Iara add up; *synonyms* (*v*) add, total, aggregate, amount, sum, tally, tot, come, number.

icembe hoe; *synonyms* (*n*) shovel, hod, adz, ladle, spatula, spool, (*v*) dig, delve, till, plow, rake, dibble, manure, tidy, turn, prepare.

iga 1. set; *synonyms* (*v*) fix, place, lay, put, locate, position, regulate, define, adjust, arrange, congeal,

posit, decline, (*n*) class, bent, circle, lot, party, repose, batch, battery, company, faction, (*adj*) fixed, fast, secure, ready, determined, establish, firm; *antonyms* (*v*) soften, liquefy, melt, (*n*) combing, comb-out, (*adj*) variable, flexible, liquid, **2.** place; *synonyms* (*n*) domicile, office, order, spot, attitude, base, job, location, situation, circumstance, center, abode, berth, dwelling, home, house, lieu, lodging, (*v*) post, rank, station, deposit, install, pitch, set, lie, commit, dispose, grade, identify; *antonym* (*v*) remove, **3.** put; *synonyms* (*v*) impose, couch, pose, charge, assign, express, make, plant, localize, aim, appoint, cast, frame, park, reckon, rest, settle, situate, stake, stand, stick, throw, submit, give, compose, bestow, do, furnish, inflict, (*n*) invest.

igai inheritance; *synonyms* (*n*) heritage, heredity, heirloom, legacy, dowry, estate, appanage, acquisition, dower, genetics, (*v*) descent.

igana hundred; *synonyms* (*n*) century, cent, centred, lathe, riding, soke, tithing, carbon, cocain, cocaine, coke, coulomb, snow, (*adj*) centigrade.

igania satisfy; *synonyms* (*v*) please, content, fill, indulge, meet, persuade, sate, satiate, appease, answer, assuage, convince, delight, execute, fulfill, gratify, serve, perform, feed, assure, compensate, discharge, fulfil, match, requite, settle, comply, cover, (*adj*) suffice, do; *antonyms* (*v*) dissatisfy, disappoint, displease, intensify.

iganIrIra 1. pile up; *synonyms* (*v*) accumulate, amass, gather, collect, hoard, conglomerate, cumulate, assemble, compile, exaggerate, garner, load, magnify, pack, **2.** stack; *synonyms* (*n*) pile, accumulation, mound, rick, mass, bunch, bundle, hill, mountain, shock, collection, haystack, batch, chimney, sheaf, smokestack, wad, bulk, cluster, drift, clump, cumulus, flock, mint, peck, (*v*) heap, lot, store, jam, cock.

igego tooth; *synonyms* (*n*) palate, grain, nap, saw, stomach, tongue, liking, fiber, point, spicule, wire, apophysis, bulb, bump, clump, condyle, dagger, dorsum, elbow, knob, node, nodosity, nodule, process, (*adj*) nib, (*v*) bite.

igIrI two; *synonyms* (*n*) deuce, pair, binary, demon, devil, duality, (*adj*) tway.

igogo crow; *synonyms* (*n*) gasconade, crowing, bragging, snigger, (*v*) boast, brag, cackle, chuckle, cry, exult, triumph, bluster, giggle, gloat, laugh, pride, titter, (*adj*) raven, charcoal.

igongona sacrifice; *synonyms* (*n*) immolation, loss, forfeiture, cost, scapegoat, victim, expense, (*v*) offering, oblation, forfeit, immolate, offer, give, lose, relinquish, grant, propose, contribute, present, victimize, devote, surrender, benefaction, boon, favor.

Igua hear; *synonyms* (*v*) attend, discover, apprehend, understand, catch, examine, learn, listen, overhear, see, try, find, get, comprehend, gather, hearken, heed, judge, receive, ascertain, attempt, determine.

iguImia hunting; *synonyms* (*n*) hunt, chase, pursuit, search, cycling, lagging, lookup, pumping, (*v*) battue, race, (*adj*) predatory.

iguku hump; *synonyms* (*n*) bump, bulge, hunch, bunch, gibbosity, knob, protuberance, swelling, jut, lump, prominence, protrusion, excrescence, extrusion, gibbousness, (*v*) bang, bed, fuck, jazz, screw, copulate, take; *antonym* (*n*) hollow.

igungu hump; *synonyms* (*n*) bump, bulge, hunch, bunch, gibbosity, knob, protuberance, swelling, jut, lump, prominence, protrusion, excrescence, extrusion, gibbousness, (*v*) bang, bed, fuck, jazz, screw, copulate, take; *antonym* (*n*) hollow.

igUrU 1. up; *synonyms* (*adv*) aloft, upward, upwardly, upwards, (*v*) raise, mount, rise, boost, advance, effervescent, filling, frothy, mousseux, nappy, sparkling, (*adj*) over, uphill, cheerful, happy, improving; *antonym* (*adj*) asleep, **2.** above; *synonyms* (*prep*) on, past, surpassing, under, (*adv*) beyond, supra, up, more, overhead, (*adj*) preceding, former, upper, foregoing, previous; *antonym* (*prep*) below, **3.** sky; *synonyms* (*n*) air, heaven, atmosphere, heavens, space, distance, (*v*) fling, flip, pitch, agitate, alternate, cant, chuck, convulse, deliver, discard, dispose, flick, gear, hawk, huckster, incline, interchange, jerk, jump, leaf, lurch, monger, peddle, riffle; **oyana igUrU** lift up.

ihiga stone; *synonyms* (*n*) jewel, rock, calculus, gem, pebble, concretion, gemstone, kernel, bullet, granite, hatchment, pitfall, plate, slug, (*v*) pit, lapidate, pelt, cake, clot.

ihindi bone; *synonyms* (*n*) os, ivory, mouth, osmium, argument, bead, block, brick, debate, discord, dispute, dissent, dollar, element, pearl, pupil, (*v*) cartilage, swot, gristle, prepare, arise, attire, beat, bill, cram, debone, drum, importune, study, (*adj*) grit.

ihIta hunting; *synonyms* (*n*) hunt, chase, pursuit, search, cycling, lagging, lookup, pumping, (*v*) battue, race, (*adj*) predatory.

ihu 1. pregnancy; *synonyms* (*n*) gravidity, gestation, fertility, behavior, childbearing, departure, doings, fetation, going, pregnance, uterogestation, traveling, ways, (*adj*) procreation, propagation, pullulation, **2.** womb; *synonyms* (*n*) uterus, belly, bowels, chitterings, cradle, entrails, guts, intestines, nest, nursery, viscera, vitals.

ihUragUri medicine man; *synonyms* (*n*) doctor, magician, vendor.

iihathatu six; *synonyms* (*n*) sise, sixer, hexad, sestet, sextet, sextuplet, ace, assize, bigness, bulk, eight, jack, king, knave, magnitude, nine, queen, seven, sextette, size, ten, deuce, five, four, sixsome, trey.

Ika do; *synonyms* (*v*) act, cheat, commit, accomplish, complete, conduct, perform, achieve, make, practice, defraud, answer, arrange, build, cause, construct, execute, play, serve, be, cut, behave, come, discharge, (*n*) function, occasion, bash, deed, (*adj*) suffice, avail; *antonyms* (*v*) neglect, unmake.

ikara 1. remain; *synonyms* (*v*) endure, bide, continue, linger, stay, keep, last, persist, live, hold, be, dwell, persevere, stand, delay, exist, reside, rest, stick, attend, lie, detain, hang, inhabit, retain, subsist, survive, tarry, prevail, (*n*) abide; *antonym* (*v*) leave, **2.** charcoal; *synonyms* (*n*) coal, fusain, anthracite, chark, culm, lignite, (*v*) carbon, coke, crayons, pastel, etching, (*adj*) soot, crow, raven, sloe, smut, black, ebony, ink, jet.

ikarathI sit; *synonyms* (*v*) model, pose, rest, ride, place, posture, put, seat, set, squat, meet, hold, convene, locate, mount, stand, settle, sprawl; *antonym* (*v*) rise.

ikinya 1. leg; *synonyms* (*n*) stage, blackleg, branch, peg, post, arm, column, limb, member, phase, rook, shank, support, fork, **2.** foot; *synonyms* (*n*) bottom, base, feet, foundation, basis, footing, measure, paw, pes, bed, butt, floor, ft, groundwork, infantry, meter, substructure, assonance, crambo, (*v*) hoof, pay, hand; *antonym* (*n*) top.

ikira 1. put; *synonyms* (*v*) place, fix, lay, position, set, impose, couch, locate, pose, charge, pitch, arrange, assign, commit, establish, express, install, make, post, plant, localize, aim, appoint, cast, frame, order, park, reckon, (*n*) deposit, invest, **2.** clothe; *synonyms* (*v*) array, dress, apparel, cover, garb, clad, deck, vest, wrap, adorn, fit, rig, bedeck, drape, furnish, garment, habilitate, indue, swathe, enclothe, (*n*) attire, habit; *antonym* (*v*) undress, **3.** wear; *synonyms* (*v*) endure, bear, fatigue, tire, waste, fray, frazzle, assume, break, don, have, last, stand, exhaust, hold, carry, sustain, chafe, rub, support, conduct, persist, sport, suffer, fag, (*n*) clothing, clothes, erosion, vesture, costume; *antonym* (*v*) refresh, **4.** place; *synonyms* (*n*) domicile, office, spot, attitude, base, job, location, situation, circumstance, center, abode, berth, dwelling, home, house, lieu, lodging, seat, standing, status, appointment, estate, (*v*) rank, station, put, lie, dispose, grade, identify, distinguish; *antonym* (*v*) remove.

ikoni bark; *synonyms* (*n*) snarl, yelp, rind, bay, crust, peel, shout, boat, barque, coat, cortex, covering, shell, ship, (*v*) yap, skin, cry, growl, roar, bellow, cough, bawl, howl, scrape, snap, woof, yell; *antonyms* (*v*) mutter, whisper.

ikoro skin; *synonyms* (*n*) peel, hide, coating, fur, hull, rind, shell, crust, integument, pelt, case, coat, covering, cutis, fell, film, fleece, teguament, exterior, outside, envelope, (*v*) pare, bark, scrape, excoriate, flay, abrade, strip, chafe, remove.

ikumi ten; *synonyms* (*n*) tenner, decade, ace, break, breath, decennary, decennium, ecstasy, female, interim, intermission, interval, jack, king, knave, methylenedioxymethamphetamine, pause, queen, recess, (*adj*) perfect, comely, desirable, faultless, glamorous, good-looking, gorgeous, meritorious, outstanding, pretty, primary.

ikundo 1. knot; *synonyms* (*n*) bow, cluster, tie, loop, bunch, gang, joint, lump, tangle, band, burl, crowd, gnarl, group, knob, node, set, twist, snag, crew, entanglement, bend, troop, (*v*) entangle, knit, bind, fasten, entwine, mass, chain, 2. bunch; *synonyms* (*n*) clump, batch, lot, horde, bulge, herd, accumulation, knot, throng, assortment, bevy, swarm, assembly, package, budget, spray, caboodle, circle, clustering, collection, flock, hump, hunch, mob, party, (*v*) bundle, huddle, pack, heap, constellate; *antonym* (*v*) disperse.

imba swell; *synonyms* (*n*) wave, dude, flow, fop, spread, growth, beau, (*v*) surge, enlarge, expand, heave, increase, rise, puff, bloat, grow, billow, augment, balloon, bulge, distend, extend, inflate, magnify, tumefy, amplify, bulk, bully, (*adj*) dandy, swagger; *antonyms* (*v*) decrease, deflate, desiccate.

ime dew; *synonyms* (*n*) condensation, mist, freshness, humidity, moisture, dag, dagger, prime, vapor, poniard, (*adj*) madefaction.

Imwe one; *synonyms* (*pron*) any, man, (*n*) anybody, single, somebody, person, ace, anyone, unit, unity, (*adj*) certain, individual, lone, only, unique, some, singular, particular, sole, united, ane, (*adv*) once.

ina sing; *synonyms* (*v*) chant, hymn, chirp, hum, drone, pipe, twitter, vocalize, carol, snitch, betray, harmonize, poetize, squeal, rat, talk, whistle, babble, blab, cheep, peach, peep, tattle, tweet, (*n*) squeak, chip.

inaina 1. shiver; *synonyms* (*n*) quiver, fragment, splinter, thrill, chill, frisson, tremor, palpitation, vibration, fright, (*v*) shake, tremble, quake, shudder, palpitate, shatter, tingle, crash, dither, smash, flutter, dash, quaver, throb, vibrate, burst, quell, (*adj*) break, crack, split, 2. shudder; *synonyms* (*n*) quivering, shivering, twitch, (*v*) shiver, flicker, jolt, shrink, pulsate, fear, jerk.

inamia turn over; *synonyms* (*v*) overturn, capsize, deliberate, give, revolve, dig, flip, roll, turn, plow, reach, invert, reverse, transfer, toss, upset, consider, debate, delve, entrust, hand, moot, pass, plough, relegate, render, think, topple, transmit.

inamIrIria 1. bend; *synonyms* (*n*) bow, arch, arc, elbow, twist, angle, curvature, bending, buckle, flexure, kink, round, (*v*) curve, turn, crouch, stoop, crook, curl, flex, deflect, fold, loop, swerve, wind, contort, cower, deform, distort, hunch, incline; *antonyms* (*v*) straighten, square, 2. hook; *synonyms* (*n*) clasp, claw, crotchet, draw, lure, trap, anchor, fastener, hand, (*v*) catch, bend, fasten, hitch, button, ensnare, attach, bag, cop, crochet, entrap,

grapple, lift, nail, secure, swipe, arrest, seize, (*adj*) lock, brace, belay, 3. twist; *synonyms* (*n*) twine, spin, twirl, entwine, braid, strain, tangle, convolution, squeeze, spiral, (*v*) coil, pervert, wrench, pull, roll, sprain, bias, entangle, intertwine, convolute, garble, meander, revolve, squirm, weave, writhe, convolve, screw, lace, enlace; *antonym* (*v*) untwist.

ingIra 1. go in; *synonyms* (*v*) enter, come, join, affiliate, arrive, ask, associate, assume, crash, deliver, don, embark, enrol, enroll, figure, immigrate, invade, request, volunteer, breach, connect, infiltrate, infix, inject, inscribe, insert, interject, interpose, introduce, participate, 2. come in; *synonyms* (*v*) disembark, aim, amount, appear, base, bulge, land, place, reply, respond, retort, return, alight, berth, commit, cross, derive, descend, direct, do, egress, emerge, enclose, erupt, estimate, fall, fare, finish, follow, grade; *antonym* (*v*) exit; **ingIra thIini** penetrate.

ingIra thIini penetrate; *synonyms* (*v*) bore, imbue, fathom, infiltrate, permeate, pierce, cut, filter, interpenetrate, enter, drill, diffuse, percolate, perforate, probe, puncture, saturate, stab, cross, move, break, strike, dig, discern, invade, sink, soak, stick, transfix, understand.

ingIrIna cohabit; *synonyms* (*v*) accustom, bed, copulate, couple, mate, conjugate, mingle.

ini liver; *synonyms* (*n*) denizen, resident.

inUrU nose; *synonyms* (*n*) beak, hooter, nozzle, proboscis, honker, bow, (*v*) pry, scent, sniff, wind, nuzzle, search, smell, snoop, poke.

inya four; *synonyms* (*n*) quaternity, foursome, quadruplet, quaternary, quaternion, tetrad, quarter, square, ace, air, appearance, cast, casting, contrivance, direction, eight, five, form, jack, king, knave, nine, quartet, quatern, queen, seven, six, ten, (*adj*) tetrarch, (*v*) warp.

inyanya eight; *synonyms* (*n*) eighter, eleven, ace, jack, king, knave, nine, octad, octet, octonary, ogdoad, queen, team, ten, ait, deuce, eightsome, five, four, octette, seven, six, trey, (*adj*) octave.

ira yesterday; *synonyms* (*n*) past, history, bygone, foretime, (*adj*) passé, stale; *antonym* (*n*) tomorrow.

iria 1. breast; *synonyms* (*n*) bosom, boob, chest, knocker, tit, titty, mammilla, bust, heart, mamma, nipple, pap, soul, spirit, teat, booby, (*v*) front, 2. lake; *synonyms* (*n*) loch, pond, pool, puddle, carmine, crimson, lin, maroon, plash, slab, tank, basin, pink, red, scarlet, vermilion, creek, lakelet, lincture, millpond, mouth, sluice, spring, (*v*) play, sport, 3. milk; *synonyms* (*v*) exploit, squeeze, drain, tap, anodyne, balm, bleed, (*adj*) albumen, chalk, glair, gluten; **iria imata** curdled milk.

iria imata curdled milk; *synonym* (*n*) bonnyclabber.

irigU banana; *synonyms* (*n*) comedian, comic, joker, nose, role, (*v*) atole, avocado, barbecue, beefsteak.

irima 1. hole; *synonyms* (*n*) cavity, aperture, crack, den, pocket, breach, break, burrow, cave, corner, depression, fix, hollow, lair, pit, vent, cavern, cranny, cell, crevice, excavation, jam, leak, opening, outlet, slit, tear, eye, nook, (*adj*) gap, **2.** nest; *synonyms* (*n*) hole, home, herd, (*v*) nestle, (*adj*) brood, hive, litter, **3.** pit; *synonyms* (*n*) dent, grave, colliery, mine, stone, dig, crater, fossa, indentation, kernel, pitfall, quarry, shaft, perforation, dimple, trench, abyss, depth, concavity, trap, vault, well, auditorium, auditory, boxes, (*v*) ditch, oppose, mark, match, pock.

iru knee; *synonyms* (*n*) elbow, genu, scythe, sickle, zigzag, angle, hinge, junction, know, stifle.

ita 1. hip; *synonyms* (*n*) haunch, coxa, loin, pelvis, (*adj*) hep, stylish, chic, in, popular, **2.** ooze out; *synonyms* (*v*) ooze, exudate, exude, transude, **3.** call; *synonyms* (*v*) cry, bellow, name, shout, bid, summon, howl, address, baptize, cite, dub, entitle, invite, scream, screech, style, title, visit, announce, bawl, arouse, ask, assemble, (*n*) appeal, yell, appoint, command, demand, request, bidding; *antonym* (*v*) dismiss, **4.** pour; *synonyms* (*v*) gush, shed, decant, flow, pelt, scatter, stream, discharge, emit, jet, run, spill, teem, effuse, deluge, funnel, swarm, tip, spout, (*n*) overflow, rain, flood; *antonym* (*v*) drizzle, **5.** leak; *synonyms* (*n*) leakage, crevice, breach, disclosure, chink, escape, fissure, hole, revelation, crack, flaw, cranny, outflow, puncture, rent, rift, seepage, (*v*) dribble, reveal, release, disclose, drip, drop, trickle, permeate, divulge, drain, filter, seep, tell.

itanga paddle; *synonyms* (*n*) blade, oar, vane, (*v*) dabble, dodder, row, pull, spank, toddle, totter, coggle, larrup.

itarara python; *synonym* (*n*) pythoness.

itarU 1. canoe; *synonyms* (*n*) boat, caique, felucca, (*adj*) self-sufficient, **2.** boat; *synonyms* (*n*) yacht, scull, craft, dinghy, ship, vessel, vehicle, shallop, schooner, sailboat, bateau, bowl, sauceboat, truck, aircraft, baiter, bucket, catamaran, clipper, dory, dragger, hulk, ketch, lifeboat, pointer, tub, umiak, (*v*) cruise.

ithangu leaf; *synonyms* (*n*) blade, page, foliage, folio, leafage, slip, (*v*) sheet, leave, flick, flip.

ithano five; *synonyms* (*n*) cinque, quint, quintuplet, fin, ace, eight, fins, fivesome, interim, intermission, interval, jack, king, knave, nine, pause, pentad, queen, quintet, recess, respite, seven, six, suspension, ten, deuce, flipper, flippers, four, (*adj*) quinary.

ithanwa axe; *synonyms* (*n*) knife, blade, (*v*) ax, chop, abort, destroy.

ithatu three; *synonyms* (*n*) leash, triplet, tercet, ternary, ternion, terzetto, third, lead, terce, tether, threesome, tierce, trey, triad, trine, trinity, trio, troika.

itigo kidney; *synonyms* (*n*) class, variety, feather, kind, nature, stripe, mettle, type, description, order, nephros, waiter.

itiki bridge; *synonyms* (*n*) span, viaduct, pontoon, tie, crossing, nosepiece, bluff, (*v*) stretch, connect, link, traverse, cross.

itimu spear; *synonyms* (*n*) harpoon, lance, pike, fizgig, gig, prick, shaft, barb, fishgig, (*v*) impale, spike, stab, pierce, skewer, stick, transfix, wound, enfilade.

itina buttocks; *synonyms* (*n*) backside, bottom, arse, ass, bum, behind, butt, nates, posterior, rear, rump, tail, anus, base, can, derriere, fanny, fundament, hindquarters, keister, prat, seat, stern, buns.

itumbI egg; *synonyms* (*n*) ball, rudiment, eggs, nut, testicle, testis, ballock, bollock, stock, bud, embryo, nucleus, addict, baseball, beginning, cell, chunk, clod, clump, crackpot, crank, germ, missile, orchis, origin, zygote, cackle, en, etymon, (*v*) nag.

itunda fruit; *synonyms* (*n*) effect, crop, outgrowth, product, consequence, issue, produce, production, yield, development, (*v*) result, return, building, edifice, erection, fabric, flower.

itura town; *synonyms* (*n*) city, borough, township, village, community, burgh, townspeople, civilization, metropolis, (*adj*) municipal, urban, local.

iya steal; *synonyms* (*v*) abstract, lift, purloin, creep, filch, misappropriate, pilfer, pinch, plunder, rob, snatch, sneak, plagiarize, slip, thieve, hook, poach, prowl, appropriate, nim, pocket, slink, swipe, take, cabbage, pussyfoot, nobble, (*n*) bargain, theft, buy.

iyuria fill; *synonyms* (*v*) block, clog, charge, line, stuff, accomplish, execute, complete, brim, close, cram, flood, fulfill, occupy, pad, plug, satisfy, stock, cloy, absorb, engage, inflate, infuse, load, meet, obstruct, (*n*) crowd, filling, packing, burden; *antonyms* (*v*) empty, free.

K

kahiU knife; *synonyms* (*n*) dagger, tongue, whittle, clapper, couteau, cuttle, cuttlefish, glossa, axe, lance, lancet, lingua, ripper, sabre, (*v*) stab, wound, jab, slit, betray, dig, murder, penetrate, puncture, trinket, gore, gouge, poke, prod, (*adj*) blade, cutlery; **kahiu ka muhuko** penknife; **kahiu ga kiuna** curved.

kama 1. milk; *synonyms* (*v*) exploit, squeeze, drain, tap, anodyne, balm, bleed, (*adj*) albumen, chalk, glair, gluten, **2.** squeeze; *synonyms* (*v*) hug, compress, pinch, embrace, extort, cram, crush, force, jam, nip, pack, squash, compact, condense, constrict, oppress, contract, crowd, cuddle, mash, pressure, push, ram, reduce, wring, narrow, screw, (n) press, grip, hold; *antonym* (v) loosen.

kamUra wring; *synonyms* (v) extort, squeeze, twist, distort, torment, torture, wrench, wrest, extract, contort, rack, twine, milk, turn, exact, force, pervert, pinch, writhe, deform, gouge, intort, (n) prick, fret, gall, grate, pierce, (adj) crimp, indent, mundify.

kanda knead; *synonyms* (v) mix, rub, form, fashion, massage, mould, shape, work, (adj) mash.

kangamia bedstead; *synonyms* (n) bed, berth, cot, bedframe, also, cradle, crib, hammock, hatch, litter, pallet, shakedown, stead, stretcher, tester, brood, development, disclosure, discovery, hatchway.

kangaUrU scorpion; *synonym* (n) cockatrice.

kanua mouth; *synonyms* (n) jaw, lip, aperture, lips, edge, entrance, brim, bill, inlet, firth, hole, nose, mouthpiece, opening, orifice, sass, verge, (v) grimace, articulate, pronounce, speak, utter, vocalize, blab, deliver, babble, declaim, talk, verbalize, accentuate; **gUtumia kanua** close.

kanyui razor; *synonyms* (n) rasour, (adj) blade, knife, cutlery, penknife, whittle.

kara deny; *synonyms* (v) contradict, controvert, decline, disavow, rebuff, abnegate, disown, gainsay, oppose, refuse, reject, renounce, abjure, contravene, disallow, disclaim, disprove, repudiate, traverse, withhold, retract, abandon, abdicate, veto, disaffirm, dispute, forbid, negate, rebut, recant; *antonyms* (v) admit, affirm, acknowledge, claim, declare, agree, maintain.

karanga fry; *synonyms* (n) chicken, child, chrysalis, cub, nestling, (v) cook, burn, singe, grill, roast, toast, electrocute, heat.

karima hill; *synonyms* (n) height, bank, gradient, mound, ascent, elevation, acclivity, embankment, grade, hillock, knoll, pile, rise, slope, hammock, heap, decline, eminence, hump, inclination, ramp, bluff, descent, incline, ridge, slant, (v) declivity, dip, stack; *antonym* (n) vale.

kenda nine; *synonyms* (n) niner, club, ennead, ace, cabaret, clubhouse, gild, golfclub, guild, jack, king, knave, lodge, nightclub, nightspot, queen, ten, deuce, eight, five, four, order, seven, six, society, trey.

keria 1. please; *synonyms* (adv) prithee, do, (v) delight, gratify, amuse, charm, entertain, like, oblige, enchant, enrapture, accommodate, divert, gladden, indulge, satisfy, suit, enthrall, tickle, take, joy, cheer, fulfill, humor, rejoice, will, wish, captivate, (adj) enjoy, content; *antonyms* (v) displease, annoy, anger, irritate, distress, **2**. satisfy; *synonyms* (v) please, fill, meet, persuade, sate, satiate, appease, answer, assuage, convince, execute, serve, perform, feed, assure, compensate, discharge, fulfil, match, requite, settle, comply, cover, keep, pay, placate, recompense, fit, slake,

(adj) suffice; *antonyms* (v) dissatisfy, disappoint, intensify.

kia grind; *synonyms* (v) labor, toil, comminute, crunch, drudge, grate, abrade, chew, crush, file, mash, scrape, sharpen, whet, bray, dig, fag, masticate, plod, rub, mince, chafe, grit, crumble, gnaw, chop, (n) mill, drudgery, struggle, work; **kImako kia ngai** awe.

kIama magic; *synonyms* (adj) magical, charming, supernatural, occult, sorcerous, witching, wizard, wizardly, mystic, (n) conjuration, incantation, charm, enchantment, legerdemain, sorcery, glamour, fascination, illusion, theurgy, trick, deception, attraction, artifice, magnetism, spell, thaumaturgy, wizardry.

kiande shoulder; *synonyms* (n) elbow, back, scale, serif, shank, (v) bear, carry, push, hold, jostle, support, sustain, assume, accept, shove, take, thrust, undertake.

kIara 1. rubbish heap; *synonym* (n) scrapheap, **2**. toe; *synonyms* (n) digit, extremity, foot, bottom, nadir, sole, adversary, antagonist, competitor, enemy, opponent, (v) toenail, (adj) toed.

kIeha 1. grief; *synonyms* (n) affliction, dolor, anguish, distress, agony, pain, regret, wound, chagrin, concern, pity, bitterness, dejection, desolation, gloom, heartbreak, melancholy, misery, remorse, sadness, sorrow, woe, disappointment, dole, compassion, ache, depression, hardship, heartache, (adj) sore; *antonyms* (n) joy, happiness, **2**. sorrow; *synonyms* (n) grief, mourning, contrition, penitence, repentance, compunction, trouble, bereavement, evil, anxiety, despair, misfortune, ruefulness, vexation, adversity, mournfulness, care, teen, annoyance, suffering, torment, torture, trial, tribulation, (v) mourn, lament, grieve, repent, rue, (adj) grievance; *antonym* (n) delight.

kiengetha hiccup; *synonyms* (n) hiccough, anomaly, fault, hitch, malfunction, problem, singultus, (v) belch.

kieni open space; *synonyms* (n) clearing, clearance, courtyard, patio, quad, quadrangle, square, dell, forecourt, forum, hall, mall.

kIero thigh; *synonym* (n) drumstick.

kIgera 1. iron ore, **2**. spring; *synonyms* (n) jump, leap, bound, fountain, skip, source, dance, rise, jet, cause, font, fount, ramp, well, run, (v) hop, caper, bounce, dive, originate, recoil, proceed, arise, issue, prance, rebound, vault, pounce, stem, (adj) elastic, **3**. machine; *synonyms* (n) instrument, apparatus, device, implement, car, contrivance, auto, automobile, gadget, organization, tool, automaton, computer, mechanism, motorcar, organ, robot, scheme, utensil, contraption, dispenser, **4**. iron; *synonyms* (n) chain, irons, chains, (v) firm, flatten, press, smooth, (adj) hard, adamant, inflexible, steel, tenacious.

kIgokora elbow; *synonyms* (*n*) bend, cubitus, angle, joint, (*v*) poke, jostle, nudge, push, shove, jolt, crowd, hustle.

kIguoya coward; *synonyms* (*n*) craven, cur, sneak, weakling, cocktail, coistril, niding, alarmist, baby, deserter, invertebrate, jellyfish, lily-liver, malingerer, nerd, pessimist, punk, quitter, scaredy-cat, shirk, shirker, yellow-belly, (*adj*) gutless, (*v*) frighten.

kIgwa sugar cane; *synonyms* (*n*) sugarcane, bamboo.

kihembe drum; *synonyms* (*n*) barrel, cask, tympan, vat, drumfish, reel, roar, tub, (*v*) beat, roll, bang, knock, pound, ram, thrum, thump, bone, cram, pulsate.

kihUmba heap; *synonyms* (*n*) pile, stack, accumulation, collection, amass, group, lot, mass, mound, bulk, bunch, congeries, gathering, batch, bundle, crowd, hoard, mint, mountain, multitude, pack, wad, aggregation, (*v*) aggregate, bank, collect, gather, accumulate, load, arrange.

kIhUni whistling; *synonyms* (*n*) whistle, pennywhistle.

kihuruta butterfly; *synonyms* (*n*) chameleon, girl, iris, lady, rainbow, spectrum, tulip, fly, (*adj*) peacock, (*v*) bray, coquet, coquette, dally, flirt, kiss, mash, philander, romance, shuttlecock, comminute, court, crunch, crush, dawdle, grind, play, solicit, squash, squeeze, squelch.

kIimba 1. corpse; *synonyms* (*n*) cadaver, carcass, body, corse, remains, stiff, clay, **2. dead person;** *synonyms* (*n*) deceased, decedent, departed, fatality.

kInato broom; *synonyms* (*n*) besom, brush, heather, ling, burbot, cusk, eelpout, swab, (*v*) sweep, filter, rake, riddle, screen, shovel, sieve, bream, cross, drag, embroil, sail, span, swing, tangle, traverse.

kIndU thing; *synonyms* (*n*) matter, affair, event, object, occurrence, article, concern, happening, something, substance, being, occasion, incident, business, deed, entity, item, episode, fad, subject, circumstance, act, issue, person, question, device, gadget, habit, part, piece.

kIngangi crocodile; *synonyms* (*n*) alligator, alacran, mosquito, octopus.

kinya 1. calabash; *synonyms* (*n*) gourd, crucible, pan, porringer, potager, saucer, dish, plate, platter, trencher, calabata, **2. arrive;** *synonyms* (*v*) come, mature, attain, fall, land, reach, succeed, show, derive, emerge, enter, get, happen, issue, prosper, disembark, (*n*) appear; *antonyms* (*v*) leave, depart, go.

kIohe 1. bundle; *synonyms* (*n*) cluster, pile, sheaf, batch, group, heap, load, package, packet, parcel, stack, wad, set, collection, lot, mass, mint, mound, mountain, roll, truss, tuft, assortment, (*v*) bunch, pack, clump, wrap, backpack, **2. pack;** *synonyms* (*n*) bundle, mob, bevy, company, herd, box, gang,

horde, knapsack, bag, flock, knot, multitude, drove, swarm, crew, band, burden, (*v*) crowd, compress, cram, fill, jam, carry, compact, crush, ram, squeeze, stuff, throng; *antonym* (*v*) unpack, **3. bale;** *synonyms* (*n*) calamity, cargo, shipment.

kionda sore; *synonyms* (*adj*) painful, sensitive, angry, raw, indignant, aching, huffy, mad, severe, tender, bitter, irritated, irritating, hurting, afflictive, (*n*) injury, boil, cut, lesion, canker, abscess, swelling, ulcer, (*v*) hurt, acute, sharp; *antonym* (*adj*) painless.

kioneki 1. vision; *synonyms* (*n*) sight, view, dream, daydream, imagination, outlook, specter, ghost, spirit, apparition, fantasy, hallucination, image, phantom, prospect, illusion, picture, shadow, foresight, spectacle, figment, idea, inspiration, show, revelation, vista, conceit, imagery, imaginativeness, (*v*) fancy; *antonym* (*n*) reality, **2. ghost;** *synonyms* (*n*) shade, soul, spectre, spook, appearance, manes, suggestion, touch, trace, vision, wraith, author, (*v*) ghostwrite, haunt.

kIongo head; *synonyms* (*n*) chief, captain, front, point, boss, foam, froth, crown, chieftain, executive, chair, brain, commander, director, end, forefront, heading, mind, president, principal, top, bow, administrator, (*adj*) foremost, great, (*v*) capital, direct, lead, command, guide; *antonyms* (*n*) subordinate, (*v*) follow.

kira be quiet; *synonyms* (*v*) silence, hush, rest, block, dummy, impede, jam, lock, obstruct, obturate, occlude, still, (*int*) soft, hold, stop.

kIraro accommodation; *synonyms* (*n*) adjustment, compromise, loan, lodging, adaptation, agreement, apartment, appeasement, convenience, ease, facility, fitting, housing, (*v*) advance, (*adj*) adaption.

kireru 1. cheek; *synonyms* (*n*) audacity, boldness, brass, face, impertinence, nerve, gall, impudence, insolence, lip, mouth, daring, disrespect, effrontery, jowl, presumption, buttock, jamb; *antonym* (*n*) respect, **2. chin;** *synonyms* (*n*) talk, jaw, jawbone, rap, mentum, button, cheek, chops, point, (*v*) speak, confer, utter.

kIrIma mountain; *synonyms* (*n*) mount, heap, height, mass, peak, pile, stack, bundle, elevation, (*v*) mound, (*adj*) lead, millstone; *antonym* (*n*) dip.

kIromo lip; *synonyms* (*n*) border, brim, cheek, edge, impertinence, mouth, rim, brink, verge, flange, impudence, backtalk, effrontery, insolence, circumference, frame, margin, shoulder, back.

kiroto dream; *synonyms* (*n*) daydream, aspiration, ambition, vision, desire, fantasy, figment, nightmare, reverie, sleep, coma, trance, notion, delusion, dreaming, phantom, conceit, (*v*) imagine, muse, contemplate, meditate, (*adj*) make-believe; *antonym* (*n*) reality.

kIruru 1. shade; *synonyms* (*n*) screen, tinge, color, ghost, hue, blind, cloud, apparition, conceal, darkness, dye, nuance, phantom, tone, look, curtain, gloom, obscurity, protect, umbrage, awning, cast, dark, dimness, (v) darken, shadow, tint, cover, obscure, overshadow; *antonyms* (n) light, brightness, **2.** shadow; *synonyms* (n) shade, tail, trace, hint, follower, reflection, silhouette, specter, spirit, satellite, shape, protection, shelter, touch, vestige, vision, attendant, conceit, (v) eclipse, follow, track, dog, hide, pursue, trail, foreshadow, chase, spy, stalk, (adj) dab.

kiugo word; *synonyms* (n) promise, news, tidings, advice, expression, intelligence, parole, password, report, statement, term, vocable, undertaking, assurance, command, communication, countersign, discussion, information, language, message, order, pledge, vow, watchword, (v) formulate, phrase, put, sentence, couch.

kIUngUyU fish; *synonyms* (n) bird, insect, mollusk, shellfish, worm, amphibian, beginner, blacktail, cob, cobnut, corkwing, dart, defense, dollar, dracunculus, dupe, excuse, (v) angle, seek, hunt, pursue, grope, rummage, beg, chowder, chupatty, clam, compote, damper, (adj) frail.

kIura frog; *synonyms* (n) frogs, toad, aigulet, anuran, batrachian, chamois, epaulet, grasshopper, abutment, dollar, freshman, goat, salientian, toadfrog, slade.

kIUru bad; *synonyms* (adj) evil, adverse, harmful, immoral, naughty, poisonous, sad, sinister, wicked, malicious, infamous, appalling, awful, damaging, devilish, disagreeable, dreadful, hurtful, ill, mischievous, nasty, negative, off, putrid, rotten, sinful, sorry, stale, (v) decayed, rancid; *antonyms* (adj) fresh, pleasant, well, well-behaved, (n) good.

koma lie down; *synonyms* (v) lie, rest, recline, repose, belong, consist, dwell, fall, lounge, relax, laze, loll, slouch, sprawl; **koma toro** sleep.

koma toro sleep; *synonyms* (n) nap, doze, kip, slumber, lie, dream, siesta, quietus, relaxation, remainder, residue, stupor, (v) rest, repose, catnap, hibernate, nod, lodge, snooze, quiet, couch, perch, recline, settle, (adj) abide.

kombera 1. lend; *synonyms* (v) loan, advance, give, grant, add, bestow, bring, contribute, impart, confer, provide; *antonym* (v) borrow, **2.** borrow; *synonyms* (v) adopt, appropriate, assume, take, accept, acquire, plagiarize, cadge, obtain, sponge, usurp, charter, copy, imitate, annex, beg, steal, absorb, arrogate, bear, cheat, creance, desume, infringe, pilfer, simulate, bite, bum, capture, (n) pledge; *antonym* (v) lend.

komera lean on; *synonyms* (v) coerce, browbeat, bully, chastise, cow, depend, dissuade, drive, enforce, exact, force, hurt, induce, intimidate, make, maul, menace, oblige, press, pressure, pressurize, push, raid, rebuke, require, squeeze, threaten, trust, harass, oppress.

konyora pound; *synonyms* (n) cage, fold, enclosure, hammering, lb, (v) beat, pen, bang, crush, flap,

grind, hammer, maul, palpitate, thump, mash, buffet, grate, baste, bruise, pulsate, pulse, ram, thrash, throb, batter, bray, drive, hit, knock.

korora cough; *synonyms* (n) coughing, sneeze, (v) choke, convulse, vomit.

kua die; *synonyms* (v) decease, dead, death, depart, expire, fall, go, pass, conk, croak, break, cease, fail, perish, sink, starve, succumb, wither, choke, decay, collapse, finish, disappear, end, exit, lapse, (n) dice, matrix, form, punch.

kUganda 1. coagulate; *synonyms* (v) clot, set, condense, congeal, harden, freeze, solidify, stiffen, (n) curdle, (adj) consolidate, coagulated, concrete, grumous; *antonym* (v) liquefy, **2.** ferment; *synonyms* (n) agitation, excitement, barm, tumult, unrest, disturbance, confusion, fermentation, fermenting, fume, restlessness, stir, turmoil, upheaval, warmth, yeast, zymosis, (v) effervesce, stew, turn, brew, fester, foam, agitate, ruffle, seethe, sour, work, (adj) pother, leaven.

kUgUra buy; *synonyms* (v) acquire, bribe, take, shop, accept, believe, get, admit, attain, corrupt, hold, obtain, procure, trade, cheap, requisition, secure, (n) bargain, purchase, acquisition, deal; *antonym* (v) sell.

kUgUrU 1. foot; *synonyms* (n) bottom, base, feet, foundation, basis, footing, measure, paw, pes, bed, butt, floor, ft, groundwork, infantry, meter, substructure, assonance, crambo, (v) hoof, pay, hand; *antonym* (n) top, **2.** leg; *synonyms* (n) stage, blackleg, branch, peg, post, arm, column, limb, member, phase, rook, shank, support, fork.

kuguuria 1. reveal; *synonyms* (v) disclose, divulge, expose, betray, convey, detect, discover, display, exhibit, express, impart, present, announce, communicate, declare, indicate, show, uncover, proclaim, find, develop, instruct, break, confess, explain, leak, manifest, open, publish, tell; *antonyms* (v) conceal, hide, cover, **2.** uncover; *synonyms* (v) unveil, reveal, strip, bare, unearth, unfold, locate, unclose, unmask, debunk, strike, ascertain, disrobe, excavate, peel, undrape, unwrap.

kuhakana border; *synonyms* (n) margin, brink, extremity, fringe, bed, boundary, brim, limit, skirt, limits, barrier, rand, confine, edging, lace, line, perimeter, periphery, (v) edge, verge, abut, adjoin, hem, surround, approach, bound, butt, enclose, flank, frame; *antonyms* (n) middle, (v) center.

kUhanana resemble; *synonyms* (v) imitate, seem, compare, correspond, agree, look, match, simulate, approximate, echo.

kUharagara 1. spread; *synonyms* (v) scatter, reach, disperse, expand, extend, broadcast, circulate, diffuse, disseminate, increase, propagate, stretch, broaden, deploy, enlarge, dilate, distribute, open, range, smear, splay, display, run, (n) span, dissemination, expanse, expansion, feast, propagation, scattering; *antonym* (*adj*) concentrated, **2.** scatter; *synonyms* (*v*) dispel, dissipate, spray, disband, sprinkle, litter, rout, dot, dust, squander, plant, intersperse, cast, lavish, disorder, break, spill, dispense, disrupt, overspread, part, shed, shower, sow, strew, (*n*) spread, dispersion, splash, sprinkling, strewing; *antonym* (*v*) gather.

kuheheta winnow; *synonyms* (*v*) fan, sift, cull, eliminate, pick, separate, glean, ventilate, examine, select, strain, weed, (*n*) winnowing, analyze, anatomize, dissect, parse, resolve, scrutinize, sifting.

kuhiha squeeze out; *synonyms* (*v*) express, eject, extrude, can, depose, discharge, dismiss, displace, distill, evict, exclude, expel, fire, gouge, release, rouse, sack, squirt, extract, terminate.

kUhinga maitho close; *synonyms* (*adj*) near, adjacent, nearby, accurate, tight, approximate, narrow, brief, airless, complete, hot, immediate, intimate, parsimonious, (*v*) compact, stop, conclude, bar, block, fold, seal, (*adv*) by, about, nigh, (*n*) end, finish, conclusion, expiration, ending, finale; *antonyms* (*adj*) distant, airy, fresh, loose, far, (*v*) open, start.

kuhingira close; *synonyms* (*adj*) near, adjacent, nearby, accurate, tight, approximate, narrow, brief, airless, complete, hot, immediate, intimate, parsimonious, (*v*) compact, stop, conclude, bar, block, fold, seal, (*adv*) by, about, nigh, (*n*) end, finish, conclusion, expiration, ending, finale; *antonyms* (*adj*) distant, airy, fresh, loose, far, (*v*) open, start.

kuhingura open; *synonyms* (*adj*) frank, obvious, artless, exposed, free, honest, bare, forthright, guileless, ingenuous, naked, direct, explicit, downright, easy, available, accessible, apparent, barefaced, blatant, conspicuous, evident, (*v*) expand, give, begin, commence, disclose, (*n*) candid, clear, loosen; *antonyms* (*adj*) devious, secretive, concealed, furtive, hidden, limited, repressive, reserved, restricted, secret, blocked, cautious, closed, crafty, enigmatic, narrow, silent, underhanded, (*v*) shut, end, finish, (*tr v*) close.

kUhinja barren; *synonyms* (*adj*) infertile, sterile, deserted, abortive, arid, dry, fruitless, meagre, stark, void, bleak, dead, desert, desolate, devoid, effete, idle, meager, poor, unfruitful, unproductive, vain, acarpous, bald, impotent, null, purposeless, (*v*) bare, lean, (*n*) waste; *antonyms* (*adj*) fertile, lush, productive.

kuhonia 1. cure; *synonyms* (*n*) remedy, antidote, medicine, salve, curative, curing, healing, therapy, treatment, restorative, aid, drug, medication, redress, relief, solution, vulcanization, (*v*) correct, help, treat, heal, pickle, preserve, restore, keep, doctor, mend, physic, recover, relieve, **2.** cool; *synonyms* (*adj*) chilly, cold, collected, composed, fine, aloof, apathetic, lukewarm, soothe, nonchalant, bracing, casual, detached,

dispassionate, distant, frigid, frosty, imperturbable, indifferent, (*v*) calm, chill, assuage, allay, pacify, quench, refrigerate, (*n*) composure, poise, aplomb, equanimity; *antonyms* (*adj*) agitated, hot, excited, enthusiastic, feverish, friendly, temperate, tepid, (*v*) warm, heat, **3.** heal; *synonyms* (*v*) cure, cicatrize, recuperate, fix, repair.

kuhoruhia bruise; *synonyms* (*n*) blow, contusion, break, buffet, swelling, blemish, mark, damage, injury, scratch, stroke, (*v*) crush, hurt, wound, beat, bray, contuse, grind, mash, pound, abrade, breach, squash, harm, injure, offend, pulverize, scrape.

kuhota 1. overcome; *synonyms* (*v*) conquer, beat, crush, subdue, vanquish, defeat, master, overpower, hurdle, overwhelm, prevail, subjugate, surmount, demolish, affect, cross, exceed, outdo, overbear, overtake, overthrow, quell, repress, suppress, triumph, trounce, (*adj*) beaten, conquered, overwhelmed, prostrate; *antonyms* (*v*) fail, (*adj*) victorious, unimpressed, **2.** vanquish; *synonyms* (*v*) overcome, rout, thrash, drub, lick, overmaster, discomfit, whip, get, reduce, tame, confound, baffle, cheat, pound, surpass, thump; *antonym* (*v*) lose, **3.** win; *synonyms* (*v*) acquire, gain, attain, obtain, achieve, earn, secure, take, succeed, carry, procure, reach, score, hit, make, receive, profit, gather, capture, accomplish, extract, finish, derive, deserve, realize, reap, seize, (*n*) profits, conquest, success.

kuhuhunyana wrinkled; *synonyms* (*adj*) furrowed, creased, crumpled, lined, puckered, wizened, wrinkly, gnarled, unironed, (*n*) rough, rugged; *antonym* (*adj*) smooth.

kuhura rub; *synonyms* (*v*) fray, grate, gall, chafe, abrade, caress, fret, furbish, graze, irritate, massage, scrape, scratch, shine, wipe, buff, file, grind, rasp, scour, scrub, scuff, touch, (*n*) check, brush, hitch, cross, hindrance, obstacle, obstruction.

kUina dance; *synonyms* (*n*) dancing, party, jerk, romp, (*v*) bound, caper, hop, bop, cavort, play, jump, shake, skip, step, beat, dandle, prance, ramp, spring, swing, trip, wave, stir.

kUinaina 1. shake; *synonyms* (*v*) beat, agitate, jar, brandish, disturb, excite, flutter, totter, wag, drop, bump, convulse, flourish, jiggle, quail, quaver, rattle, rock, shiver, stir, trill, (*n*) tremble, jolt, quiver, wave, trembling, shudder, tremor, wiggle, (*adj*) quake, **2.** tremble; *synonyms* (*v*) shake, thrill, palpitate, falter, flicker, vibrate, waver, cower, fear, wobble, blench, cringe, didder, flinch, recoil, shrink, (*n*) throb, tingle, heave, pant, (*adj*) crumble, starve.

kUiyUra abound; *synonyms* (*n*) exuberate, (*v*) swarm, flow, teem, burst, overflow.

kumbata grasp; *synonyms* (*n*) grip, catch, clasp, clutch, clinch, appreciation, apprehension, clutches, comprehension, reach, (*v*) comprehend, embrace, hold, apprehend, grapple, conceive, capture, cling, grab, clench, compass, dig, sense, snatch, understand, digest, fathom, gather, absorb, appreciate; *antonym* (*v*) release.

kumbuka fly; *synonyms* (*v*) escape, dash, drive, flee, glide, elope, aviate, dart, flutter, hop, hover, hurry, jet, race, run, rush, shoot, soar, speed, tear, wave, balloon, desert, bolt, (*n*) flap, (*adj*) break, flit, burst, insect, bounce.

kumera grow; *synonyms* (*v*) advance, augment, develop, enlarge, expand, come, emerge, become, farm, get, rise, spring, turn, breed, accrue, arise, blossom, evolve, extend, flourish, germinate, increase, mature, raise, sprout, thrive, go, enhance, cause, climb; *antonyms* (*v*) decrease, weaken, shrink.

kundika plait; *synonyms* (*n*) fold, braid, pigtail, plat, pleat, tuck, plication, pucker, tress, twist, (*v*) lace, crease, entwine, double, interlace, intertwine, plight, ply, twine, weave, mat.

kungania 1. collect; *synonyms* (*v*) assemble, accumulate, amass, gather, pick, accrue, acquire, aggregate, cluster, collate, congregate, convene, cull, harvest, hoard, raise, accept, catch, compile, derive, flock, gain, garner, glean, group, levy, marshal, meet, muster, obtain; *antonyms* (*v*) disperse, distribute, **2.** assemble; *synonyms* (*v*) call, collect, concentrate, converge, make, rally, edit, arrange, build, construct, erect, piece, pile, combine, form, convoke, create, fabricate, foregather, forgather, frame, join, mass, organize, rendezvous, sit, summon, unite, manufacture, prepare; *antonyms* (*v*) dismantle, disband, disassemble.

kUnja 1. forge; *synonyms* (*n*) smith, smithy, (*v*) counterfeit, falsify, devise, fabricate, fake, fashion, coin, contrive, invent, mint, construct, excogitate, feign, form, hammer, mold, mould, shape, build, copy, frame, imitate, make, manufacture, weave, work, cast, formulate, **2.** twist; *synonyms* (*n*) twine, wind, spin, twirl, entwine, braid, kink, loop, strain, tangle, convolution, crook, (*v*) turn, bend, distort, curl, coil, contort, deform, curve, pervert, wrench, pull, roll, sprain, bias, entangle, intertwine, convolute, garble; *antonyms* (*v*) straighten, untwist, **3.** bend; *synonyms* (*n*) bow, arch, arc, elbow, twist, angle, curvature, bending, buckle, flexure, round, curving, sweep, bob, (*v*) crouch, stoop, flex, deflect, fold, swerve, cower, hunch, incline, sag, submit, sway, tilt, tip, curb, fork; *antonym* (*v*) square.

kunora 1. sharpen; *synonyms* (*v*) focus, edge, hone, intensify, point, sharp, increase, heighten, whet, improve, compound, stimulate, taper, incite, kindle, quicken, (*n*) aim; *antonym* (*v*) cloud, **2.** thick; *synonyms* (*adj*) dense, compact, stupid, crowded, dull, heavy, opaque, slow, stocky, close, deep, dim, familiar, fat, gross, intimate, muddy, obtuse, solid, broad, impenetrable, concentrated, dumb, populous, frequent, chummy, coarse, hazy,

intense, (*n*) midst; *antonyms* (*adj*) thin, intelligent, bright, sparse, clever, diluted, fine, slight, transparent, **3.** fat; *synonyms* (*adj*) stout, corpulent, thick, bulky, fatty, fertile, fleshy, gainful, greasy, great, obese, overweight, plump, rich, big, ample, chubby, hefty, juicy, lucrative, (*n*) avoirdupois, blubber, cream, fatness, grease, lard, oil, (*v*) fatten, bloated, exaggerated; *antonyms* (*adj*) slim, skinny, slender.

kunungira 1. smell out; *synonyms* (*v*) detect, locate, trace, track, **2.** sniff; *synonyms* (*v*) scent, inhale, nose, smell, snuff, breathe, whiff, sniffle, smoke; *antonym* (*v*) exhale.

kunyita 1. held; *synonyms* (*adj*) absorbed, confined, alleged, assumed, believed, bound, caged, captive, detained, fast, immersed, obsessed, occupied, protected, rapt, reputed, responsible, restrained, rumored, said, secured, spellbound, supposed, tenable, thought, trapped, understood, whispered, available, (*adv*) on, **2.** arrest; *synonyms* (*n*) stop, check, halt, apprehension, custody, hold, detention, standstill, stay, stoppage, glom, arrestation, cessation, confinement, control, (*v*) capture, catch, apprehend, collar, delay, detain, get, hinder, inhibit, nail, obstruct, retard, hook, block, contain; *antonyms* (*v*) release, discharge, **3.** seize; *synonyms* (*v*) grab, arrest, clutch, grapple, receive, annex, assume, clasp, confiscate, conquer, grasp, grip, carry, appropriate, commandeer, impound, perceive, tackle, take, kidnap, abduct, intercept, snap, adopt, obtain, affect, attach, captivate, occupy, (*n*) snatch.

kuogotha wind up; *synonyms* (*v*) finish, end, terminate, wind, close, complete, cease, conclude, hoist, agitate, arouse, excite, provoke, raise, sex, shake, stimulate, stir, stop; *antonym* (*v*) undo.

kuoha mIrigo pack; *synonyms* (*n*) bundle, mob, bevy, bunch, company, herd, batch, backpack, box, gang, horde, package, knapsack, cluster, bag, flock, group, knot, lot, multitude, (*v*) crowd, compress, heap, cram, fill, jam, load, carry, compact, crush; *antonym* (*v*) unpack.

kuora rotten; *synonyms* (*adj*) bad, foul, poor, fetid, lousy, musty, off, putrid, ill, shabby, corrupt, crappy, decomposed, sour, stinking, terrible, mean, vicious, low, decomposing, treacherous, atrocious, cheap, contemptible, despicable, dirty, (*v*) decayed, rancid, weak, effete; *antonym* (*adj*) fresh.

kUra old; *synonyms* (*adj*) antiquated, obsolete, ancient, former, aged, antique, elderly, experienced, outdated, veteran, archaic, decrepit, hoary, mature, past, stale, disused, hackneyed, late, traditional, decayed, inveterate, auld, gray, musty, olden, older, outmoded, previous, primitive; *antonyms* (*adj*) new, young, modern, fresh, latest, novel, original, youthful.

kurarama 1. roar; *synonyms* (*n*) boom, thunder, shout, bark, noise, peal, clamor, roll, bang, bellowing, blast, hollo, (v) bellow, cry, bawl, howl, clatter, blare, call, holler, rave, scream, yell, growl, screech, shriek, storm, wail, (adj) bluster, rage; antonym (v) whisper, **2.** rumble; synonyms (n) roar, mutter, brawl, buzz, report, riot, rumbling, rumor, uproar, fight, fighting, grumbling, (v) murmur, grumble, sound, mumble, drone, resound, drum, snarl, (adj) row.

kUratha set; synonyms (v) fix, place, lay, put, locate, position, regulate, define, adjust, arrange, congeal, posit, decline, (n) class, bent, circle, lot, party, repose, batch, battery, company, faction, (adj) fixed, fast, secure, ready, determined, establish, firm; antonyms (v) soften, liquefy, melt, (n) combing, comb-out, (adj) variable, flexible, liquid.

kuregera 1. weak; synonyms (adj) feeble, frail, faint, flat, flimsy, fragile, thin, watery, light, ailing, cowardly, delicate, diluted, exhausted, inadequate, infirm, lax, nerveless, poor, shaky, sickly, slack, slight, soft, decrepit, powerless, effeminate, impotent, (v) loose, (n) helpless; antonyms (adj) strong, brave, concentrated, firm, safe, compelling, determined, effective, forceful, healthy, intense, powerful, resolute, robust, sturdy, vigorous, able, fit, hard-wearing, loud, **2.** faint; synonyms (adj) collapse, dim, dizzy, indistinct, weak, dull, gentle, vague, distant, drop, fuzzy, hazy, languid, low, mild, obscure, subtle, groggy, confused, subdued, debilitated, tired, blurry, cold, fainthearted, (v) languish, swoon, droop, conk, pale; antonyms (adj) distinct, clear, obvious, considerable, pungent.

kUrIkia 1. decisive; synonyms (adj) conclusive, critical, crucial, decided, definite, final, important, positive, authoritative, convincing, definitive, determined, peremptory, vital, deciding, clean, certain, confident, explicit, fatal, fateful, key, last, (v) absolute, categorical, determinate, unequivocal, unqualified, clear, (n) effectual; antonyms (adj) indecisive, uncertain, unsure, weak, **2.** final; synonyms (adj) decisive, extreme, latter, ultimate, irrevocable, concluding, eventual, net, firm, dying, ending, finished, fixed, hindmost, later, parting, resolved, supreme, terminal, unconditional, utmost, utter, back, completing, irrefutable, (n) examination; antonyms (adj) first, opening, preliminary.

kurIma cultivate; synonyms (v) civilize, educate, grow, produce, train, advance, breed, crop, develop, domesticate, farm, improve, raise, refine, prepare, dig, cherish, discipline, encourage, form, forward, foster, further, nurse, nurture, plow, school, (adj) promote, sharpen, (n) manure; antonym (v) neglect.

kUringIka faint; synonyms (adj) collapse, dim, dizzy, feeble, indistinct, weak, dull, gentle, soft, vague, delicate, distant, drop, fuzzy, hazy, languid, light, low, mild, obscure, sickly, subtle, groggy, confused, (v) languish, swoon, droop, conk, exhausted, pale;

antonyms (adj) distinct, strong, clear, obvious, considerable, loud, pungent.

kurira 1. disappear; synonyms (v) die, vanish, melt, fade, depart, dematerialize, sink, go, pass, end, abscond, fall, scram, disperse, dissolve, escape, evaporate, lift, perish, leave; antonyms (v) appear, stay, **2.** fade; synonyms (v) disappear, decline, wither, discolor, droop, drop, languish, expire, decay, diminish, dwindle, evanesce, flag, wane, weaken, wilt, deteriorate, decrease, dim, bleach, fail, faint, lessen, pale, recede, reduce, shrink, shrivel, (n) disappearance, (adj) stale; antonyms (v) grow, increase, strengthen.

kuruka rest; synonyms (n) remnant, repose, balance, pause, recess, relaxation, residue, leisure, break, quiet, respite, halt, intermission, interval, (v) nap, remain, sleep, ease, lie, perch, abide, recline, relief, stay, dwell, lean, depend, breathe, (adj) remainder, remains; antonym (v) work.

kuruma 1. creep; synonyms (v) crawl, grovel, sneak, steal, fawn, lurk, cringe, sidle, slip, truckle, cower, edge, itch, pussyfoot, tingle, (n) crawling, creeping, sycophant, toady, **2.** crawl; synonyms (v) creep, clamber, climb, scramble, swarm, teem, inch, lag, move, swim, crawfish; antonym (v) race.

kururia 1. drag; synonyms (v) attract, haul, draw, puff, trail, cart, hale, heave, lug, tow, delay, shamble, delineate, dredge, force, inhale, lag, rake, shuffle, sweep, train, (n) puller, bother, bore, hindrance, inhalation, friction, clog, pressure, track; antonym (v) push, **2.** pull; synonyms (v) drag, draught, pluck, jerk, tug, pick, make, lure, strain, get, appeal, arrest, commit, extract, stretch, tear, yank, charm, drive, extend, (n) wrench, attraction, effort, twist, influence, control, allure, tension, exertion, fascination; antonym (v) repel.

kUrUta 1. scrape; synonyms (v) scratch, graze, rub, pare, rake, grate, mark, abrade, chafe, grind, claw, engrave, file, fray, rasp, scour, skin, squeak, dent, skimp, clean, grave, scoop, (n) score, abrasion, predicament, difficulty, quagmire, dilemma, cut, **2.** grace; synonyms (n) elegance, favor, clemency, beauty, benediction, blessing, charm, benefit, forgiveness, pity, charity, comeliness, goodwill, mercy, (v) bedeck, adorn, deck, garnish, beautify, decorate, embellish, dress, embroider, enrich, dignify, bedight, ornament, (adj) goodness, beneficence, kindness, **3.** scratch; synonyms (n) nick, scrabble, groove, scar, furrow, excoriation, gash, line, rip, scraping, scribble, zero, bread, gouge, blot, (v) notch, scrape, scrawl, tear, itch, slash, split, gall, burrow, hurt, obliterate, blemish, break, (adj) bruise, buffet, **4.** grate; synonyms (n) lattice, fireplace, grating, grid, grill, grille, (v) creak, fret, gnash, aggravate, annoy, crunch, irritate, provoke, grit, bother, jar, rankle, rile, scuff, bray, drudge.

kuua 1. take; *synonyms* (*v*) admit, get, hold, adopt, bear, carry, catch, clutch, obtain, return, borrow, pick, acquire, appropriate, assume, bring, capture, claim, convey, demand, grab, have, interpret, require, select, steal, swallow, (*n*) seize, (*phr*) accept, receive; *antonyms* (*v*) give, refuse, abstain, add, lose, **2**. carry; *synonyms* (*v*) conduct, take, acquit, behave, comport, pack, transport, load, act, cart, channel, contain, deport, ferry, handle, haul, impress, keep, lug, move, run, shoulder, stock, support, sustain, sway, transfer, transmit, waft, accomplish.

kuunamirira 1. lean; *synonyms* (*adj*) emaciated, gaunt, thin, bony, lank, lanky, scrawny, flimsy, angular, barren, haggard, meager, skinny, slender, spare, (*v*) incline, bend, list, slant, bow, careen, pitch, slope, tip, gravitate, angle, loll, recline, (*n*) tilt, inclination; *antonyms* (*adj*) fat, plump, **2**. slope; *synonyms* (*n*) declivity, dip, decline, descent, fall, grade, gradient, hill, brae, hillside, ramp, rise, drop, side, declination, declension, falling, talus, (*v*) cant, lean, bank, descend, sway, oblique, lurch, (*adj*) obliquity.

kUUra dwell; *synonyms* (*v*) abide, inhabit, reside, bide, live, stay, lodge, be, belong, brood, continue, delay, occupy, remain, settle, consist, domicile, domiciliate, endure, exist, keep, last, lie, people, ponder, populate, shack, tarry, aby, (*adj*) roost.

kuuraga 1. break; *synonyms* (*v*) split, crack, burst, fail, infringe, leak, tear, undo, beat, bust, chip, contravene, fold, interrupt, part, (*n*) breach, fracture, pause, rupture, stop, collapse, interruption, respite, suspension, breakage, chance, defeat, gap, hiatus, lull; *antonyms* (*v*) repair, obey, honor, mend, (*n*) continuation, **2**. snap; *synonyms* (*v*) bite, break, nip, clack, snarl, rap, rip, rive, click, flick, shoot, rend, bolt, dash, flip, bark, (*n*) photograph, catch, go, picnic, pushover, clasp, cinch, grab, shot, snatch, pep, picture, fastening, kick.

kuuruga 1. stir; *synonyms* (*v*) arouse, budge, move, rouse, affect, agitate, excite, inspire, go, cause, foment, shift, actuate, animate, awaken, beat, disturb, (*n*) movement, commotion, disturbance, excitement, agitation, fuss, riot, tumult, ferment, ado, din, disorder, (*adj*) bustle, **2**. stir up; *synonyms* (*v*) incite, instigate, stimulate, stir, fan, inflame, provoke, raise, awake, anger, ignite, prod, shake, irritate, mix, enkindle, encourage, commove, evoke, heat, kindle, light, motivate, remind, roil, wake, whip, (*adj*) sharpen; *antonyms* (*v*) calm, dampen.

kuurugira stir up; *synonyms* (*v*) incite, arouse, excite, instigate, stimulate, stir, awaken, agitate, disturb, fan, foment, inflame, provoke, raise, awake, inspire, move, rouse, anger, ignite, prod, shake, irritate, mix, enkindle, encourage, commove, evoke, heat, kindle; *antonyms* (*v*) calm, dampen.

kwagana wicked; *synonyms* (*adj*) atrocious, bad, evil, sinful, vicious, depraved, immoral, mischievous, unholy, vile, corrupt, criminal, diabolical, foul, hellish, iniquitous, nasty, naughty, pernicious, ungodly, impious, perverse, base, black, dark, despicable, devilish, diabolic, disgusting, dissolute; *antonyms* (*adj*) good, innocent, kind, moral, pious, pure.

kwanIrIria take in; *synonyms* (*v*) comprehend, absorb, admit, deceive, embrace, fool, take, contain, adopt, dupe, get, have, imbibe, receive, assimilate, see, apprehend, hold, cheat, gull, recognize, grasp, involve, learn, make, observe, realize, understand, attract, beguile.

kwenda 1. want; *synonyms* (*v*) need, desire, require, like, hope, crave, covet, (*n*) lack, poverty, wish, deficiency, deprivation, famine, absence, dearth, demand, destitution, indigence, necessity, penury, privation, shortage, pauperism, defect, requirement, distress, ambition, fancy, essential, hardship; *antonyms* (*v*) dislike, hate, **2**. love; *synonyms* (*n*) affection, dear, fondness, liking, benevolence, charity, attachment, beloved, darling, devotion, honey, sweetheart, favor, beau, adoration, friendship, passion, pet, regard, tenderness, amour, heart, partiality, (*v*) cherish, enjoy, worship, adore, affect, treasure, (*adj*) flame; *antonyms* (*n*) abhorrence, hatred, aversion, (*v*) abhor, **3**. need; *synonyms* (*v*) claim, involve, exact, have, take, ask, necessitate, acquire, entail, ought, should, accept, blame, (*n*) want, must, beggary, exigency, motive, impoverishment, obligation, urge, impulse, occasion, compulsion, drought, force, misery, neediness, prerequisite, use; *antonym* (*n*) wealth, **4**. wish; *synonyms* (*v*) aspiration, choose, please, bid, care, prefer, intend, mean, trust, long, decide, (*n*) inclination, longing, aim, pleasure, purpose, craving, mind, request, dream, plan, thirst, goal, hunger, petition, wishing, compliments, hankering, object, (*adv*) will.

kwendia sell; *synonyms* (*v*) peddle, deal, handle, betray, give, promote, deceive, exchange, merchandise, realize, trade, vend, clear, gammon, pass, deliver, negotiate, distribute, push, transfer, (*n*) cheat, fake, hoax, shave, pitch; *antonym* (*v*) buy.

kwenya shave; *synonyms* (*v*) prune, clip, pare, reduce, scrape, cut, brush, chip, crop, shear, whittle, graze, mow, peel, plane, slice, trim, lower, slash, strip, attenuate, file, grind, reap, (*n*) shaving, (*adj*) lop, dock.

kwIgangara dance; *synonyms* (*n*) dancing, party, jerk, romp, (*v*) bound, caper, hop, bop, cavort, play, jump, shake, skip, step, beat, dandle, prance, ramp, spring, swing, trip, wave, stir.

kwihutia abstain; *synonyms* (*v*) refrain, desist, avoid, forbear, cease, decline, eschew, withhold, fast; *antonym* (*v*) consume.

kwIrua ripen; *synonyms* (*v*) mature, grow, maturate, ripe, age, season, cultivate, develop, elaborate, fructify, (*adj*) perfect.

kwirUta learn; *synonyms* (*v*) discover, get, know, find, ascertain, have, hear, determine, acquire, con, perceive, study, tell, understand, gather, assimilate, instruct, read, see, teach, absorb, catch, follow, detect, establish, comprehend, memorize, remember, take, assume.

kwiyoga bathe; *synonyms* (*v*) wash, steep, tub, bath, clean, immerse, rinse, soak, plunge, water, dip, douse, dunk, imbathe, wet, saturate, (*n*) swim, (*adj*) lave.

kwogothithama wind up; *synonyms* (*v*) finish, end, terminate, wind, close, complete, cease, conclude, hoist, agitate, arouse, excite, provoke, raise, sex, shake, stimulate, stir, stop; *antonym* (*v*) undo.

M

macamanio 1. crossroads; *synonyms* (*n*) junction, parting, articulation, center, contingency, hamlet, juncture, pass, pinch, join, joint, occasion, village, **2.** bifurcation; *synonyms* (*n*) fork, forking, furcation, divergence, split, division.

maguta oil; *synonyms* (*n*) petroleum, fat, ointment, salve, cream, fuel, cerate, lotion, (*v*) lubricate, anoint, anele, glycerine.

mahatha twin; *synonyms* (*adj*) dual, matching, identical, similar, two, indistinguishable, (*n*) match, counterpart, mate, pair, fellow, parallel, brother, equivalent, pendant, second, similitude, (*v*) double, duplicate, equal, couple, geminate, concomitant.

mahUha 1. boil; *synonyms* (*v*) seethe, bubble, churn, simmer, ferment, burn, effervesce, fume, heat, anger, gurgle, cook, foam, froth, roast, (*n*) abscess, blister, furuncle, pimple, boiling, bump, eruption, pustule, swelling, seed, (*adj*) sore, rave, fester, stew, ulcer; *antonym* (*v*) freeze, **2.** abscess; *synonyms* (*n*) boil, gathering, growth, aposteme, blemish, bulge, bunion, distension, engorgement, enlargement, excrescence, eyesore, imposthumation, imposthume, inflammation, puffiness, spot, wound, assembly, collection, congregation, crowd, lesion, monstrosity, suppuration.

mahuti 1. hay; *synonyms* (*n*) fodder, feed, bunk, food, silage, hedge, meal, pasture, **2.** garbage; *synonyms* (*n*) debris, filth, waste, litter, refuse, hooey, rubbish, scrap, scraps, drivel, twaddle, (*adj*) trash; *antonym* (*v*) sense, **3.** rubbish; *synonyms* (*n*) garbage, nonsense, junk, offal, hogwash, trumpery, dirt, falderal, absurdity, folderol, rubble, balderdash, bull, codswallop, rot, tripe, wreckage, applesauce, (*adj*) bosh.

maI 1. water; *synonyms* (*n*) urine, moisture, juice, liquor, crystal, glass, lymph, pee, piddle, piss, vitrite, (*v*) irrigate, moisten, wet, soak, dampen, dilute, (*adj*) soundings, **2.** excrement; *synonyms* (*n*) dejection, faeces, dirt, evacuation, dung, excretion, ordure, excreta, (*adj*) feces, **3.** dung; *synonyms* (*n*) compost, droppings, excrement, filth, muck; **gutaha maI** draw.

maIndU affair; *synonyms* (*n*) matter, business, concern, event, job, occasion, occurrence, amour, duty, happening, incident, issue, party, subject, theme, thing, topic, transaction, meeting, affaire, case, circumstance, episode, experience, fact, function, liaison, occupation, relationship, (*v*) collision.

maithori tears; *synonyms* (*n*) cry, crying, brine, lacerations, lament, moan, pickle, snuffle, weeping.

maitu mother; *synonyms* (*n*) mamma, parent, (*v*) father, beget, engender, generate, care, sire, fuss, get; **mUrUwa maitU** relative.

makia 1. startle; *synonyms* (*v*) alarm, frighten, jump, scare, astonish, shock, astound, amaze, shake, dismay, electrify, rouse, stagger, terrify, disturb, panic, jolt, appall, daunt, dumbfound, stun, agitate, fluster, galvanize, originate, perturb, ruffle, (*n*) start, leap, (*adv*) surprise, **2.** threaten; *synonyms* (*v*) menace, bully, endanger, intimidate, loom, offer, imperil, jeopardize, peril, approach, foreshadow, portend, browbeat, impend, coerce, terrorize, augur, await, betoken, domineer, forebode, foretell, presage, undermine, (*n*) threat; *antonym* (*v*) help, **3.** jerk; *synonyms* (*n*) tug, heave, pull, fool, dork, jog, idiot, jerking, plunge, (*v*) yank, jar, twitch, fling, bump, flip, bob, bounce, convulse, draw, flick, hitch, recoil, buck, cast, chuck, flinch, haul, pitch, pluck, snap.

makunU mushroom; *synonyms* (*n*) fungus, parvenu, upstart, beige, gent, (*v*) expand, spread, burgeon, flourish, grow, proliferate, thrive; *antonym* (*v*) decrease.

mambarita thatched roof; *synonyms* (*n*) thatch, teach.

manyamaro 1. hardship; *synonyms* (*n*) adversity, distress, calamity, affliction, grievance, difficulty, trouble, burden, disaster, asperity, deprivation, destitution, misfortune, poverty, suffering, trial, catastrophe, hardness, strait, misery, neediness, pain, penury, pressure, rigour, severity, sorrow, want, grimness, rigor; *antonym* (*n*) affluence, **2.** distress; *synonyms* (*n*) agony, anguish, anxiety, grief, hurt, torture, alarm, disquiet, ache, shock, agonize, bitterness, damage, desolation, dismay, exigency, (*v*) afflict, torment, concern, bother, upset, worry, discomfort, annoy, distraint, ail, disturb, embarrass, grieve, harass; *antonyms* (*v*) comfort, please.

mata spittle; *synonyms* (*n*) saliva, slaver, spit, sputum, expectoration, slabber, spattle, spatula, spawl, spet, spitting, spital, tongue; **tua mata spit.**

mathuguno urine; *synonyms* (*n*) piss, pee, water, piddle, emiction, lanterloo, netting, peeing, pissing, weewee.

matu cloud; *synonyms* (*n*) mist, blur, haze, steam, cloak, blind, crowd, curtain, film, flock, gloom, pall, (*v*) fog, becloud, obscure, befog, blacken, eclipse, overshadow, shadow, taint, hide, impair, dim, mottle, overcast, shade, sully, (*adj*) swarm, muddy; *antonym* (*v*) sharpen.

mbakI tobacco; *synonyms* (*n*) baccy, nicotian, (*adj*) nicotine.

mbara war; *synonyms* (*n*) combat, battle, fight, warfare, conflict, fighting, antagonism, contest, struggle, opposition, contention, enmity, campaign, encounter, hostilities, hostility, skirmish, (*v*) clash, (*adj*) military; *antonyms* (*n*) peace, (*v*) ceasefire.

mbarathi horse; *synonyms* (*n*) cavalry, mount, buck, heroin, junk, knight, boar, cock, dog, drake, gander, hart.

mbari clan; *synonyms* (*n*) family, tribe, breed, house, kin, kindred, lineage, race, stock, genus, company, gang, class, faction, folk, fraternity, line, people, set, species, stem, stirps, trunk, association, brotherhood.

mbata 1. grasp; *synonyms* (*n*) grip, catch, clasp, clutch, clinch, appreciation, apprehension, clutches, comprehension, reach, (*v*) comprehend, embrace, hold, apprehend, grapple, conceive, capture, cling, grab, clench, compass, dig, sense, snatch, understand, digest, fathom, gather, absorb, appreciate; *antonym* (*v*) release, **2.** duck; *synonyms* (*n*) darling, canvas, dear, love, blackcock, (*v*) dip, douse, plunge, dodge, circumvent, dive, evade, souse, bob, avoid, crouch, dunk, elude, hedge, parry, shirk, skirt, stoop, submerge, cut, bow, fudge, shun, sidestep, (*adj*) immerse.

mbegu 1. sperm; *synonyms* (*n*) seed, semen, spermatozoon, germ, birth, bud, children, descendants, egg, embryo, etymon, gemmule, generation, nucleus, offspring, origin, original, progeny, race, radicle, root, source, spermatozoan, stem, stirps, stock, trunk, **2.** seed; *synonyms* (*n*) issue, posterity, brood, beginning, berry, breed, core, cum, spawn, ejaculate, litter, spike, (*v*) inseminate, plant, sow, (*adj*) crumb, bit, cantlet, flitter, gobbet, inch, mite, morsel, patch, scantling.

mbogo buffalo; *synonyms* (*n*) bison, yak, zebu, buffalofish, bugle, husband, cat, dog, (*v*) cow, bully, frighten, intimidate, baffle, deceive, foil, get, impress, mystify, nonplus, perplex, puzzle, stump, unnerve; **mbogo kenyarare** tsetse fly.

mbogo kenyarare tsetse fly; *synonyms* (*n*) glossina, tsetse, tzetze.

mbombo pump; *synonyms* (*n*) heart, pumps, ticker, (*v*) interrogate, draw, examine, milk, question.

mbuku hare; *synonyms* (*n*) rabbit, cony, puss, cat, coney, maukin, lapin, malkin, (*v*) excite, harry, (*adj*) antelope, courser, eagle, gazelle, greyhound, chickaree, chipmunk, hackee, ostrich, scorcher, squirrel.

mbura rain; *synonyms* (*n*) precipitation, wet, pelting, flow, rainfall, rainwater, abound, exuberate, mist, teem, (*v*) pour, stream, hail, precipitate, shower, condense, pelt, sprinkle.

mbUri goat; *synonyms* (*n*) butt, lecher, satyr, chamois, fornicator, gallant, grasshopper, paillard, arse, ass, backside, behind, bottom, bum, buns, buttocks, can, cigaret, cigarette, derriere, dweeb, fag, fanny, flunkey, flunky, fool, fundament, intrigant, laughingstock, milk.

mena 1. hate; *synonyms* (*v*) abhor, detest, abominate, loathe, despise, scorn, disdain, (*n*) dislike, enmity, abhorrence, animosity, detestation, hatred, abomination, antipathy, aversion, distaste, execration, hostility, loathing, odium, revulsion, spite, disgust, grudge, rancor, repugnance, repulsion, venom; *antonyms* (*v*) love, like, adore, **2.** detest; *synonyms* (*v*) hate, execrate, nauseate.

menya know; *synonyms* (*v*) discern, comprehend, can, distinguish, have, recognize, understand, feel, acknowledge, agnise, agnize, apprehend, fathom, appreciate, cognize, experience, get, grasp, perceive, realize, see, endure, hear, differentiate, interpret, place, recognise, taste, (*n*) ken, notice.

menyerera 1. look after; *synonyms* (*v*) keep, guard, attend, defend, maintain, protect, control, care, nurse, nurture, preserve, safeguard, save, tend, watch; *antonym* (*v*) neglect, **2.** take care; *synonyms* (*v*) mind, beware, see, look, examine, heed, appear, consider, expect, face, front, seem, **3.** care for; *synonyms* (*v*) cherish, fancy, like, love, treat, affect, raise.

meria swallow; *synonyms* (*v*) eat, bolt, gulp, consume, devour, accept, absorb, bear, endure, stomach, brook, gobble, gorge, engulf, abide, bury, engross, imbibe, immerse, pocket, suffer, tolerate, believe, (*n*) drink, sip, swig, taste, deglutition, mouthful, sup; *antonym* (*v*) regurgitate.

mIeU yawn; *synonyms* (*n*) yawning, nod, (*v*) gape, open, ope, yaw.

mIrukI 1. gas; *synonyms* (*n*) gasoline, petrol, air, fumes, accelerator, flatulence, petroleum, oil, gasolene, vapor, flatulency, (*v*) fuel, brag, vaunt, blague, blow, bluff, bluster, boast, crow, **2.** vapour; *synonyms* (*n*) evaporation, gas, vaporisation, vaporization, dehydration, desiccation.

moca weak; *synonyms* (*adj*) feeble, frail, faint, flat, flimsy, fragile, thin, watery, light, ailing, cowardly, delicate, diluted, exhausted, inadequate, infirm, lax, nerveless, poor, shaky, sickly, slack, slight, soft, decrepit, powerless, effeminate, impotent, (v) loose, (n) helpless; *antonyms* (adj) strong, brave, concentrated, firm, safe, compelling, determined, effective, forceful, healthy, intense, powerful, resolute, robust, sturdy, vigorous, able, fit, hard-wearing, loud.

mUcamo taste; *synonyms* (n) bit, flavor, liking, morsel, penchant, appetite, drink, drop, fondness, gusto, mouthful, predilection, preference, refinement, style, bite, discrimination, judgment, elegance, sapidity, sense, palate, (v) relish, savor, sample, smack, discernment, touch, try, gust; *antonyms* (n) dislike, tastelessness.

mUciarithania midwife; *synonyms* (n) accoucheuse, accoucheur, oculist, howdy, (v) midwive.

mucii home; *synonyms* (n) fireside, abode, domicile, house, base, building, dwelling, family, habitation, household, place, residence, shelter, asylum, fatherland, habitat, lodging, lodge, land, environment, accommodation, address, homeland, housing, mansion, menage, (adj) domestic, internal, interior, national.

mUcinga gun; *synonyms* (n) artillery, gunman, handgun, ordnance, pistol, revolver, shooter, torpedo, accelerator, arrow, gas, (v) shoot, cracker.

mUcuthi tail; *synonyms* (n) rear, shadow, behind, butt, posterior, rump, stub, backside, bottom, buttocks, stern, arse, ass, bum, end, fanny, train, bait, (v) follow, pursue, track, trail, chase, dog, tag, bob, dock, spy, stalk, (adj) back; *antonyms* (v) head, front.

mUgambo voice; *synonyms* (n) speech, sound, language, part, suffrage, vote, vox, ballot, mouthpiece, representative, mouth, articulation, election, interpreter, plebiscite, poll, spokesperson, vocalization, (v) enunciate, express, pronounce, say, speak, utter, vocalize, articulate, state.

mUgate bread; *synonyms* (n) living, livelihood, cash, maintenance, currency, dough, food, kale, loot, money, pelf, sustenance.

mUgathi bead; *synonyms* (n) drop, astragal, beading, pearl, dot, beadwork, bubble, drip, droplet, globule, (v) beautify, adorn.

mUgeni 1. stranger; *synonyms* (n) alien, foreigner, outsider, newcomer, outlander, unknown; *antonyms* (n) associate, friend, native, pal, **2.** guest; *synonyms* (n) stranger, caller, customer, visitor, client, visitant.

mUgogo bridge; *synonyms* (n) span, viaduct, pontoon, tie, crossing, nosepiece, bluff, (v) stretch, connect, link, traverse, cross.

mUgUnda 1. garden; *synonyms* (n) field, bed, orchard, grounds, park, patch, plaisance, plot, garth, lawn, backyard, court, cemetery, close, croft, enclosure, meadow, outdoors, precincts, stadium, (v) farm, cultivate, (adj) commonplace, familiar,

ordinary, average, everyday, humdrum, nondescript, outdoor, **2.** land; *synonyms* (n) ground, country, soil, kingdom, domain, estate, nation, realm, state, empire, commonwealth, demesne, property, dirt, area, (v) disembark, debark, alight, get, drop, arrive, bring, down, perch, secure, acquire, impose, capture, convey, fall; *antonym* (adj) aquatic.

muguongo 1. ivory; *synonyms* (n) bone, tusk, dentin, elephant, bead, drop, pearl, yellow, os, (adj) chalk, lily, milk, paper, pearly, snow, white, **2.** trunk; *synonyms* (n) stem, boot, torso, body, bole, proboscis, snout, stalk, box, stock, case, house, luggage, nose, stirps, **3.** horn; *synonyms* (n) hooter, cornet, klaxon, alarm, trumpet, aparejo, arm, faldstool, ophicleide, trombone, cup, beak, basin, bellcrank, bowl, chalice, flask, glass, goblet, honker, jorum, (v) butt, cuckold, detusk, hornify, (adj) bulb, bullet, clew, globule, knob.

mugwanja seven; *synonyms* (n) heptad, septet, ace, eight, jack, king, knave, nine, queen, septette, ten, deuce, five, four, sevensome, six, trey.

mUgwI arrow; *synonyms* (n) pointer, barb, bolt, dart, missile, gun, spear, javelin, jereed, jerid, lance, pike, projectile, spontoon, swallowtail, boomerang, gaff, harpoon, marker, pin, (adj) rocket, hydrargyrum, quicksilver.

muhaka boundary; *synonyms* (n) border, bound, limit, edge, area, end, perimeter, periphery, barrier, brink, fringe, frontier, line, margin, outskirts, rim, verge, bounds, circuit, circumference, compass, division, edging, extremity, limitation, pale, precinct, restriction, side, term.

muhane smallpox; *synonym* (n) variola.

muhari 1. line; *synonyms* (n) cord, file, house, breed, course, family, lineage, field, ancestry, border, boundary, cable, crease, row, stock, trace, way, birth, band, business, channel, crinkle, furrow, job, mark, path, pedigree, (v) order, wrinkle, edge, **2.** row; *synonyms* (n) altercation, line, rank, squabble, wrangle, clash, dispute, turmoil, argument, chain, conflict, fray, hassle, noise, stir, tiff, uproar, clamor, contest, (v) quarrel, brawl, fight, argue, bicker, broil, oar, pull, range, (adj) fracas, riot; *antonyms* (n) agreement, (v) agree.

muhUyU foam; *synonyms* (n) froth, spume, bubbles, lather, (v) boil, bubble, effervesce, seethe, fizz, suds, ferment, churn, gurgle, rage, storm, (adj) fume.

muici thief; *synonyms* (n) robber, burglar, bandit, pirate, plunderer, crook, filcher, stealer, despoiler, freebooter, pillager, rifler.

muigwa thorn; *synonyms* (n) spine, barb, bramble, prickle, spike, point, needle, pricker, sticker, bristle, fang, irritant, (adj) sting, cancer.

mUirItu 1. girl; *synonyms* (n) damsel, lady, daughter, fille, lass, maid, wench, virgin, quean, female, girlfriend, woman, **2.** virgin; *synonyms* (adj) pure, vestal, chaste, innocent, new, fresh, intact, untouched, unmixed, virginal, virtuous, unmarried, (*n*) maiden, girl.

muitirira giraffe; *synonyms* (*n*) camelopard, (*adj*) giant, grenadier.

mUkamo udder; *synonyms* (*n*) bag, pericarp, bagful, base, dish, grip, handbag, pocketbook, purse, suitcase.

mukebe 1. metal pot, **2.** pot; *synonyms* (*n*) caldron, boiler, can, bucket, belly, cannabis, commode, container, flowerpot, grass, heap, jug, pan, pile, pool, urn, kitty, pickle, basin, bowl, ganja, hemp, jar, marihuana, (*v*) bottle, cure, (*adj*) deal, marijuana, volume, hashish, **3.** mug; *synonyms* (*n*) countenance, pot, chump, cup, face, kisser, sucker, tankard, victim, fool, mugful, phiz, physiognomy, pitcher, visage, photograph, (*v*) rob, grimace, attack, steal.

mUkiha vein; *synonyms* (*n*) streak, vena, nervure, strain, mine, temper, stripe, tone, cast, style, fund, funicle, stock, (*adj*) humor, mood, strip.

mukonyo navel; *synonyms* (*n*) bellybutton, center, umbilicus, nave, omphalos, omphalus.

mUku ashes; *synonyms* (*n*) dust, cinder, cinders, remains, clay, embers, body, cadaver, clinker, corpse, defunct, relics, reliquiae, carcass, coals, ember, residue, skeleton, (*adj*) mother, precipitate, scoriae.

mUkuanju stick; *synonyms* (*n*) bar, club, rod, bat, cane, cudgel, (*v*) adhere, stab, attach, cling, fix, paste, staff, cohere, affix, bind, cleave, fasten, hold, impale, persist, pink, spear, spike, cement, join, put, poke, gore, spit.

mukummuthu backbone; *synonyms* (*n*) back, guts, strength, bottom, courage, grit, mainstay, nerve, pluck, spine, stamina, character, fortitude, mettle, pillar, rachis, spirit, support, anchor, (*adj*) core, gist, marrow, pith, quiddity, quintessence.

mUndU person; *synonyms* (*n*) fellow, human, individual, man, being, body, character, creature, mortal, soul, life, homo, form, organism, personality, somebody, someone, substance, thing, partner, (*v*) party; *antonym* (*n*) automaton; **mUndU witU** relative; **mUndU mwithI** youth; **mundu mweru** white man; **mUndU mUkUrU** old person; **mUndU mUka mUtumia** wife.

mUndU mUkUrU old person; *synonym* (*n*) oldster.

mUndU mwithI youth; *synonyms* (*n*) boy, juvenile, lad, young, youngster, adolescence, kid, juvenility, puberty, stripling, younker, child, puppy, infancy, childhood, guy, prime, youthfulness, fellow, teenager, (*adj*) adolescent; *antonyms* (*n*) adulthood, adult, ripeness.

mUndU witU 1. relative; *synonyms* (*adj*) related, comparative, proportionate, proportional, dependent, relevant, (*n*) relation, brother,

connection, congenator, congener, (*v*) kinsman; *antonym* (*adj*) absolute, **2.** brother; *synonyms* (*n*) fellow, pal, associate, buddy, chum, companion, compeer, comrade, counterpart, crony, friend, mate, monk, peer, sidekick, equal; *antonym* (*n*) sister.

mUnene 1. chief; *synonyms* (*adj*) head, principal, cardinal, capital, arch, central, essential, first, main, primary, sovereign, basic, dominant, especial, foremost, grand, important, key, leading, (*n*) administrator, boss, captain, executive, leader, paramount, superior, top, chieftain, commander, director; *antonyms* (*adj*) minor, associate, secondary, **2.** great; *synonyms* (*adj*) eminent, famous, gigantic, big, distinguished, extensive, extreme, large, chief, ample, celebrated, considerable, dignified, fantastic, fine, glorious, good, massive, spacious, voluminous, stunning, vigorous, wide, admirable, almighty, bulky, dandy, deep, elevated, enormous; *antonyms* (*adj*) small, awful, insignificant, tiny, mild, **3.** powerful; *synonyms* (*adj*) cogent, able, brawny, forcible, hard, mighty, muscular, potent, strong, effective, energetic, influential, intense, lusty, hardy, full, formidable, hefty, robust, stiff, sturdy, valid, convincing, husky, athletic, fit, dynamic, efficacious, efficient, (*n*) fierce; *antonyms* (*adj*) powerless, weak, **4.** master; *synonyms* (*n*) instructor, gentleman, authority, employer, headmaster, maestro, overlord, professional, sir, skipper, teacher, conqueror, host, boy, (*v*) conquer, control, command, defeat, dominate, overcome, subdue, subjugate, surmount, govern, bridle, check, (*adj*) original, ace, expert, proficient.

mUnyongoro 1. centipede, **2.** millipede; *synonyms* (*n*) millepede, milliped.

mUnyU salt; *synonyms* (*n*) salinity, sal, blunt, cream, dust, mopus, rhino, (*adj*) salty, saline, briny, spice, pungent, season, (*v*) cure, pickle, embalm.

muramba banana; *synonyms* (*n*) comedian, comic, joker, nose, role, (*v*) atole, avocado, barbecue, beefsteak.

murango door; *synonyms* (*n*) gate, threshold, access, doorway, entrance, entry, mouth, opening, entryway, exit, hatch, inlet, porch, portal, wicket, chops, covercle.

mUrari soot; *synonyms* (*n*) smut, grime, lampblack, crock, coom, dirt, collow, dust, filth, soil, stain, grunge, (*v*) ash, cinder, embers, scoriae, (*adj*) smoke, ink, ebony, jet, soote.

mUri root; *synonyms* (*n*) base, foundation, origin, basis, radical, radix, cause, derivation, reason, beginning, bottom, core, essence, etymon, heart, source, stem, groundwork, germ, stub, foot, nub, fountain, parent, (*v*) establish, dig, fix, grub, rummage, burrow.

murigo 1. load; *synonyms* (*n*) charge, cargo, freight, stack, heap, pack, weight, consignment, lading, shipment, strain, anxiety, care, crowd, encumbrance, loading, mass, onus, pressure, (*v*) burden, fill, encumber, pile, lade, stow, glut, cram, laden, overload, saddle; *antonym* (*v*) unload, **2.** burden; *synonyms* (*n*) load, bale, concern, core, essence, gist, imposition, liability, millstone, responsibility, worry, stress, distress, cark, chorus, curse, difficulty, duty, (*v*) bother, burthen, clog, trouble, afflict, force, handicap, impose, hamper, impede, blame, (*adj*) blow; *antonyms* (*v*) relieve, unburden.

mUrio 1. sweet; *synonyms* (*adj*) beloved, delicious, fresh, lovely, mellow, dear, lovable, melodious, musical, pleasant, pleasing, sugary, charming, delightful, fragrant, honeyed, luscious, odorous, savory, aromatic, clean, amiable, cute, dainty, dulcet, gentle, (*n*) confection, confectionery, darling, dessert; *antonyms* (*adj*) sour, acid, bitter, discordant, acidic, pungent, sharp, salty, **2.** pleasant; *synonyms* (*adj*) bright, acceptable, agreeable, jolly, kindly, nice, facetious, affable, attractive, cheerful, clear, comfortable, congenial, enjoyable, fair, fine, genial, joyful, joyous, kind, mirthful, pretty, delectable, mild, jocular, suave, amusing, beautiful, clement, convivial; *antonyms* (*adj*) unpleasant, disagreeable, disgusting, foul, gruesome, harsh, horrible, nasty, repugnant, shocking, terrible, unwelcome, appalling, frosty, grisly, rough.

mUrIro 1. cry; *synonyms* (*n*) shout, bark, scream, yell, clamor, roar, bay, crying, buzz, exclamation, groan, hearsay, noise, report, rumor, sob, (*v*) call, bellow, shriek, weep, exclaim, howl, moan, outcry, screech, yelp, yowl, holler, hollo, squawk; *antonyms* (*v*) laugh, whisper, **2.** sound; *synonyms* (*n*) echo, peal, audio, (*v*) ring, chime, fast, blow, chirp, boom, enunciate, fathom, plumb, probe, resound, seem, (*adj*) reasonable, complete, healthy, fit, good, just, rational, right, sane, sensible, robust, certain, firm, hearty, solid; *antonyms* (*n*) silence, (*adj*) illogical, unsound, confused.

murogi sorcerer; *synonyms* (*n*) magician, enchanter, necromancer, conjurer, wizard, conjuror.

mUrUme husband; *synonyms* (*n*) consort, wife, hubby, man, master, mate, partner, spouse, baron, (*v*) conserve, economize, preserve, save, economise.

mUrUthi lion; *synonyms* (*n*) celebrity, cat, curiosity, luminary, spectacle, name, notable, leader, magnate, (*adj*) hero, worthy, somebody, tiger, eminent, noted.

mUrUwa maitU 1. relative; *synonyms* (*adj*) related, comparative, proportionate, proportional, dependent, relevant, (*n*) relation, brother, connection, congenator, congener, (*v*) kinsman; *antonym* (*adj*) absolute, **2.** brother; *synonyms* (*n*) fellow, pal, associate, buddy, chum, companion, compeer, comrade, counterpart, crony, friend, mate, monk, peer, sidekick, equal; *antonym* (*n*) sister.

mutaro 1. groove; *synonyms* (*n*) furrow, rut, chamfer, ditch, cut, track, crease, custom, fissure, hollow, line, notch, rabbet, sulcus, wrinkle, dike, trough, fold, drain, duct, habit, routine, scratch, slot, trench, gash, (*v*) channel, flute, score, gouge, **2.** furrow; *synonyms* (*n*) crinkle, pucker, ridge, dent, gutter, seam, (*v*) groove, chase, crumple, plough.

mutego 1. trap; *synonyms* (*n*) snare, net, ambush, gin, mesh, noose, entanglement, ambuscade, bait, hole, deception, artifice, bunker, dogcart, (*v*) catch, entrap, ensnare, trick, entangle, capture, decoy, hook, immobilize, lure, seize, get, enmesh, confine, hold, bag, **2.** snare; *synonyms* (*n*) trap, pitfall, temptation, trapan, (*v*) allurement, springe, pilfer.

muthaiga 1. remedy; *synonyms* (*n*) cure, redress, medicine, drug, relief, antidote, curative, medication, physic, remediation, salve, therapy, treatment, amendment, amends, restorative, prescription, assistance, correction, (*v*) heal, help, amend, rectify, correct, relieve, aid, doctor, reform, fix, mend, **2.** medicine; *synonyms* (*n*) medicament, remedy, cathartic, potion, preparation, (*v*) medicate.

muthamaki king; *synonyms* (*n*) emperor, mogul, sovereign, chief, baron, crown, magnate, ruler, tycoon, majesty, rex, monarch, power, ace.

mUthandUkU smallpox; *synonym* (*n*) variola.

mUthenya 1. day; *synonyms* (*n*) light, daylight, generation, age, daytime, epoch, time, crisis; *antonyms* (*n*) nighttime, night, **2.** daytime; *synonyms* (*n*) day, sunshine.

muthia 1. tip; *synonyms* (*n*) top, hint, peak, point, pinnacle, apex, bribe, clue, crown, gratuity, suggestion, summit, extremity, reward, pitch, advice, baksheesh, counsel, crest, edge, end, head, height, (*v*) incline, tilt, dump, lean, slant, list, cap, **2.** utmost; *synonyms* (*adj*) extreme, farthest, last, supreme, uttermost, furthest, highest, greatest, ultimate, farthermost, most, outermost, paramount, final, terminal, chief, main, (*n*) maximum, best, furthermost, limit, **3.** top; *synonyms* (*adj*) superlative, first, foremost, major, superior, upper, utmost, (*n*) acme, cover, surface, brow, covering, lid, tip, lead, pate, prime, culmination, roof, side, (*v*) exceed, outdo, surpass, beat, better, climax, excel, pass, outstrip, transcend; *antonyms* (*adj*) worst, (*n*) bottom, base, nadir, **4.** peak; *synonyms* (*n*) mountain, bill, bloom, flush, heyday, highlight, vertex, visor, zenith, apogee, nib, altitude, meridian, ridge, blossom, efflorescence, elevation, extremum, eyeshade, flower, (*adj*) cliff, bluff, optimum, tor; *antonym* (*n*) trough, **5.** point; *synonyms* (*n*) place, grade, aim, article, degree, dot, mark, spot, phase, detail, matter, moment, position, particular, barb, gist, goal, instant, item, meaning, period, regard, (v) direct, level, betoken, charge, focus, guide, indicate, show, **6.** highest point; *synonym* (n) ceiling.

mUthiIne movement; *synonyms* (n) motion, move, action, activity, campaign, crusade, advancement, cause, drive, passage, drift, flow, inclination, effort, evolution, front, migration, play, progress, tendency, travel, course, gesture, act, impulse, maneuver, behavior, development, exercise, gait.

muthimimo heel; *synonyms* (n) blackguard, counter, dog, cad, scoundrel, shoe, sole, villain, bounder, (v) list, lean.

mUthita penis; *synonyms* (n) member, phallus, appendage, extremity.

muthonge hut; *synonyms* (n) cabin, cot, booth, hovel, cottage, hutch, lodge, shanty, shed, shack, shelter, stall.

mUtI 1. handle; *synonyms* (v) administer, conduct, feel, wield, control, deal, direct, finger, manage, manipulate, touch, treat, govern, cope, grope, ply, process, stock, work, apply, exercise, administrate, (n) grip, clutch, grasp, haft, handgrip, hold, knob, ear, **2.** tree; *synonyms* (n) gallows, gibbet, stem, house, tribe, hierarchy, landmark, lentisk, ranking, trunk, filler, (v) corner, collar, **3.** haft; *synonyms* (n) handle, helve, hilt, heft, key, tiller, treadle, trigger, dwelling.

mutingoe tail; *synonyms* (n) rear, shadow, behind, butt, posterior, rump, stub, backside, bottom, buttocks, stern, arse, ass, bum, end, fanny, train, bait, (v) follow, pursue, track, trail, chase, dog, tag, bob, dock, spy, stalk, (adj) back; *antonyms* (v) head, front.

mUtitU forest; *synonyms* (n) timber, jungle, woodland, timberland, wood, woods, (v) afforest.

mUtuithania judge; *synonyms* (n) arbiter, arbitrator, referee, connoisseur, critic, (v) consider, estimate, evaluate, think, believe, condemn, assess, adjudicate, calculate, decide, guess, umpire, examine, conceive, adjudge, conclude, deem, esteem, gauge, hold, review, suppose, try, measure, assume.

mUtuma woman; *synonyms* (n) wife, girl, maid, womanhood, char, charwoman, soul, (obj) female, she; *antonyms* (n) man, gentleman.

mUtwe head; *synonyms* (n) chief, captain, front, point, boss, foam, froth, crown, chieftain, executive, chair, brain, commander, director, end, forefront, heading, mind, president, principal, top, bow, administrator, (adj) foremost, great, (v) capital, direct, lead, command, guide; *antonyms* (n) subordinate, (v) follow.

mUUru bad; *synonyms* (adj) evil, adverse, harmful, immoral, naughty, poisonous, sad, sinister, wicked, malicious, infamous, appalling, awful, damaging, devilish, disagreeable, dreadful, hurtful, ill,

mischievous, nasty, negative, off, putrid, rotten, sinful, sorry, stale, (v) decayed, rancid; *antonyms* (adj) fresh, pleasant, well, well-behaved, (n) good.

mUUthI pestle; *synonyms* (n) pounder, muller, stamp, cast, impression, mold, muser, crusher, grinder, implement, ponderer, postage, rod, ruminator, seal, utensil, (v) grind, powder, pound.

mwaka year; *synonyms* (n) twelvemonth, day, age, time, yr, class, hour, minute, month, quarter, second, week.

mwaki fire; *synonyms* (n) discharge, ardor, conflagration, explode, fervor, flame, bonfire, burning, enthusiasm, energy, barrage, ardour, (v) excite, eject, blaze, dismiss, ignite, kindle, expel, animate, arouse, burn, inflame, light, provoke, sack, shoot, stimulate, stir, send; *antonym* (v) hire.

mwana child; *synonyms* (n) baby, boy, babe, bairn, brat, girl, infant, juvenile, kid, minor, toddler, tot, youngster, innocent, imp, daughter, descendant, individual, nestling, offspring, progeny, scion, son, tike, tyke, lad; *antonym* (n) adult.

mwanake young man; *synonyms* (n) beau, boyfriend, lad, fellow, associate, blighter, buster, chap, clotheshorse, colleague, companion, comrade, confrere, cuss, dandy, dude, familiar, fella, feller, fop, gallant, gent, sheik, (adj) swain, lover, admirer, adorer, follower, inamorato, suitor.

mwathi master; *synonyms* (n) captain, instructor, head, boss, leader, gentleman, authority, employer, headmaster, maestro, overlord, professional, sir, skipper, teacher, conqueror, (v) conquer, control, command, defeat, dominate, overcome, subdue, subjugate, surmount, (adj) chief, original, ace, expert, proficient.

mwene self; *synonyms* (n) ego, person, being, individual, someone, character, essence, individuality, personality, selfness, soul, spirit, (adj) same.

mweri moon; *synonyms* (n) lunation, moonlight, moonshine, satellite, epoch, bootleg, posterior, rump, (v) daydream, dream, fantasize, bemuse, gaze, glare, meditate, mope, mull, muse, ponder, sulk, desire, languish, stargaze, woolgather, (adj) quicksilver, weathercock; **utheri wa mweri** moonlight.

mwIgere kanio imitate; *synonyms* (v) copy, duplicate, forge, ape, emulate, follow, feign, counterfeit, mimic, mock, act, assume, echo, model, pattern, pretend, reproduce, sham, simulate, adopt, parody, represent, fake, impersonate, mirror, replicate, resemble, apply, appropriate, parallel.

mwIiko oar; *synonyms* (n) sail, screw, blade, (v) row.

mwIrI body; *synonyms* (n) cadaver, corpse, matter, organization, carcass, cluster, consistency, figure, mass, set, aggregate, association, entity, amount, bulk, company, corps, creature, flesh, form, frame, fuselage, group, individual, material, mob, mortal, party, person, quantity; *antonym* (n) spirit.

N

naigUrU upright; *synonyms* (*adj*) perpendicular, straight, erect, vertical, fair, good, just, righteous, honest, honorable, plumb, right, true, virtuous, pure, clean, moral, noble, respectable, standing, sound, bolt, faithful, proper, reliable, worthy, blameless, (*n*) column, pillar, post; *antonyms* (*adv*) horizontally, (*adj*) disreputable, prone, upturned, degenerate, hanging, unwholesome.

narua haste; *synonyms* (*n*) celerity, expedition, rapidity, rush, speed, bustle, hastiness, quickness, velocity, alacrity, speediness, swiftness, diligence, (*v*) hurry, dash, dispatch, hasten, hustle; *antonym* (*n*) slowness.

nda 1. pregnancy; *synonyms* (*n*) gravidity, gestation, fertility, behavior, childbearing, departure, doings, fetation, going, pregnance, uterogestation, traveling, ways, (*adj*) procreation, propagation, pullulation, **2.** belly; *synonyms* (*n*) abdomen, stomach, inside, bowels, intestines, waist, entrails, gut, paunch, venter, (*v*) balloon, swell, billow, bloat, bulge, **3.** stomach; *synonyms* (*n*) appetite, belly, breadbasket, inclination, maw, relish, taste, hunger, palate, tummy, (*v*) accept, brook, abide, bear, endure, stand, suffer, take, tolerate, support, go, hold, lump, allow, sustain, withstand, (*adj*) digest, swallow, eat, pocket.

ndaa louse; *synonyms* (*n*) worm, insect, cad, miscreant, morpion, nuisance, scoundrel, sneak, mite, rascal, rogue, tick, (*adj*) vermin.

ndaya long; *synonyms* (*adj*) extended, lengthy, dragging, far, oblong, diffuse, farseeing, farsighted, foresighted, foresightful, (*v*) aspire, desire, hanker, languish, yearn, ache, hunger, wish, crave, pine, yen, want, (*n*) extensive, large; *antonyms* (*adj*) short, brief.

ndegwa 1. bull; *synonyms* (*n*) bullshit, bunk, hogwash, rot, absurdity, bear, buck, buncombe, bunkum, cop, copper, crap, fuzz, guff, male, nonsense, pig, shit, (*adj*) blunder, **2.** heifer; *synonyms* (*n*) calf, cow, shorthorn, query.

nderi eagle; *synonyms* (*n*) colors, labarum, oriflamb, oriflamme, aviator, flag, pilot, streamer, (*adj*) antelope, chickaree, chipmunk, courser, doe, gazelle, greyhound, hackee, hare, ostrich, scorcher, squirrel.

nderu beard; *synonyms* (*n*) awn, hair, whiskers, disguise, sloven, (*v*) dare, defy, camouflage, mask, (*adj*) brave.

ndia pool; *synonyms* (*n*) plash, lake, pond, mere, cartel, basin, kitty, syndicate, trust, billiards, lough, store, bank, jackpot, loch, association, deep, pot, puddle, reservoir, well, baths, broad, consortium, (*v*) combine, merge, associate, consolidate, amalgamate, unite.

ndigiri donkey; *synonyms* (*n*) burro, ass, fool, idiot, moke, jackass, simpleton, dizzard.

ndimbo 1. snail; *synonyms* (*n*) escargot, dodman, hodmandod, testudo, (*v*) sluggard, lingerer, loiterer, tortoise, **2.** slug; *synonyms* (*n*) bullet, shot, loafer, projectile, scale, serif, shank, shoulder, signature, swig, (*v*) smash, wallop, slog, beat, strike, punch, whack, hit, idle, laze, (*adv*) crawl, creep, lag.

ndinoho snail; *synonyms* (*n*) escargot, dodman, hodmandod, testudo, (*v*) sluggard, lingerer, loiterer, tortoise.

nditU 1. serious; *synonyms* (*adj*) grave, heavy, sedate, austere, great, hard, considerable, critical, dangerous, earnest, grievous, sad, sober, bad, big, deep, major, severe, solemn, weighty, devout, acute, consequential, dull, grand, grim, pressing, (*v*) important, momentous, demure; *antonyms* (*adj*) frivolous, lighthearted, cheerful, flippant, humorous, mild, minor, playful, slight, **2.** heavy; *synonyms* (*adj*) dark, dense, fat, full, gross, arduous, bulky, burdensome, oppressive, thick, compact, ample, awkward, cumbersome, grueling, overweight, ponderous, sluggish, sound, strong, sullen, torpid, corpulent, fleshy, cloudy, languid, close, dreary, firm, (*n*) drowsy; *antonyms* (*adj*) light, easy, slim, thin, gentle, puny, skinny, **3.** dull; *synonyms* (*adj*) dim, blunt, bland, boring, cold, dismal, inactive, inert, obtuse, slack, slow, stupid, uninteresting, apathetic, commonplace, dingy, drab, flat, glassy, humdrum, lifeless, tame, tiresome, backward, hollow, bald, (*v*) deaden, dampen, damp, monotonous; *antonyms* (*adj*) bright, lively, sharp, exciting, interesting, lustrous, stimulating, amusing, exhilarating, glittery, glossy, glowing, high-pitched, intense, luminous, shiny, sparkling, varied, brisk, bubbly, clear, distinctive, imaginative, inspiring, risk-taking.

ndogo smoke; *synonyms* (*n*) fumes, fog, mist, perfume, smoking, smoulder, vapor, weed, bullet, cannabis, fastball, heater, hummer, pot, (*v*) fume, reek, fumigate, puff, exhale, cure, burn, smolder, evaporate, (*adj*) smudge, tobacco, blot, blur, daub.

ndoro 1. mire; *synonyms* (*n*) bog, filth, marsh, dirt, quagmire, muck, sludge, tangle, morass, ooze, slush, swamp, (*v*) involve, entangle, (*adj*) mud, **2.** mud; *synonyms* (*n*) grime, soil, (*adj*) clay, (*v*) mire.

nduma darkness; *synonyms* (*n*) dark, night, shade, shadow, blindness, duskiness, gloom, murk, cloud, cloudiness, dimness, gloominess, iniquity, mirk, murkiness, obscurity, secrecy, wickedness, concealment; *antonyms* (*n*) light, brightness, lightness; **nduma njirU** dark.

nduma njirU 1. dark; *synonyms* (*adj*) black, dismal, cheerless, dim, obscure, blind, blue, deep, gloomy, murky, mysterious, sable, abstruse, cryptic, thick, benighted, bleak, dingy, disconsolate, dull, dusky, grim, morose, (*n*) cloudy, darkness, evening, night, shadow, confused, gloom; *antonyms* (*adj*) bright, sunny, fair, clear, pale, pallid, sunlit, (*n*) light, day, **2**. black; *synonyms* (*adj*) dark, blackamoor, darkie, dirty, ebony, evil, nigger, unclean, squalid, desolate, disgraceful, fateful, ignominious, inglorious, inky, muddy, opprobrious, shameful, somber, sullen, swarthy, ugly, achromatic, (*n*) blackness, mourning, (*v*) sinister, villainous, blacken; *antonym* (*n*) white.

ndurul 1. below; *synonyms* (*adv*) beneath, under, down, infra, downstairs, (*prep*) underneath, (*adj*) low, after; *antonyms* (*prep*) above, over, **2**. underneath; *synonyms* (*prep*) below, (*n*) bottom, (*adj*) inferior.

negenania quarrel; *synonyms* (*n*) brawl, feud, altercation, dissension, clash, conflict, difference, disagreement, argument, contention, controversy, debate, fracas, misunderstanding, breach, fray, fuss, (*v*) dispute, fight, argue, row, disagree, squabble, wrangle, affray, altercate, bicker, contest, disturbance, scrap; *antonyms* (*n*) agreement, (*v*) agree.

nene 1. large; *synonyms* (*adj*) big, ample, extensive, generous, broad, bulky, considerable, handsome, high, heavy, abundant, capacious, great, gross, hefty, huge, important, roomy, stout, fat, bountiful, colossal, commodious, comprehensive, copious, enormous, expansive, fair, full, giant; *antonyms* (*adj*) small, cramped, insignificant, **2**. great; *synonyms* (*adj*) eminent, famous, gigantic, distinguished, extreme, grand, large, chief, capital, celebrated, dignified, fantastic, fine, glorious, good, massive, spacious, voluminous, stunning, vigorous, wide, admirable, almighty, dandy, deep, elevated, exalted, excellent, frightful, groovy; *antonyms* (*adj*) awful, tiny, mild.

nengera give; *synonyms* (*v*) allow, bestow, extend, accord, commit, donate, contribute, convey, deliver, dispense, endow, grant, present, yield, administer, apply, bequeath, bring, cast, communicate, concede, dedicate, devote, distribute, do, exhibit, gift, leave, supply, serve; *antonyms* (*v*) withdraw, take, withhold.

ngagatu bitter; *synonyms* (*adj*) acrimonious, biting, acrid, sharp, acerbic, acid, caustic, keen, malicious, resentful, sour, virulent, acerb, cutting, freezing, harsh, icy, inclement, pungent, raw, sarcastic, severe, tart, unpleasant, venomous, austere, angry, astringent, (*n*) acerbity, (*v*) disagreeable; *antonyms* (*adj*) mild, sweet, charitable, hot, kind, sugary.

ngambucu jaw; *synonyms* (*n*) chin, jaws, mandible, talk, (*v*) chatter, gossip, chat, gab, jabber, berate, chaffer, chew, confabulate, gabble, chide, lecture, masticate, natter, rebuke, reprimand, reproof, scold, visit, yack, blabber, chitchat, (*adj*) clack, palaver, prate, prattle.

Nganga guinea fowl; *synonyms* (*n*) dago, greaseball, wop.

ng'araga hunger; *synonyms* (*n*) desire, thirst, appetite, craving, wish, itch, eagerness, famine, longing, starvation, yen, greed, hankering, hungriness, malnutrition, passion, yearning, keenness, voracity, (*v*) crave, want, ache, long, lust, yearn, covet, famish, languish, starve, envy; *antonym* (*n*) moderation.

ngarI leopard; *synonyms* (*n*) cat, marble, nacre, ocelot, opal, ophite, pard, libbard, pardale, zebra.

ngigi locust; *synonyms* (*v*) losel, squanderer.

ngima 1. porridge; *synonyms* (*n*) gruel, broth, loblolly, plash, podge, puddle, (*v*) oatmeal, chowder, chupatty, clam, compote, damper, fish, frumenty, grapes, lettuce, mango, mangosteen, oyster, pineapple, salmis, sauerkraut, succotash, supawn, trepang, vanilla, waffle, walnut, **2**. monk; *synonyms* (*n*) monastic, hermit, conventual, priest, cenobite, abbot, monkey, palmer, pilgrim, cleric, justice, minister, nun, parson, preacher, prior, recluse, rector, religieux, reverend, vicar, solitary.

ngingo neck; *synonyms* (*n*) throat, cervix, neckline, lapel, beard, col, (*v*) pet, cut, love, manage, kiss, behead, bang, bed, bonk, caress, come, complete, comprehend, contend, cope, deal, discern, distinguish, do, eff, fare, fondle, (*adj*) stricture, wasp.

ngitI dog; *synonyms* (*n*) cur, andiron, blackguard, click, detent, cad, cock, heel, pawl, bounder, (*v*) chase, hound, beset, hunt, tail, track, trail, course, follow, persecute, pursue, shadow, tag, attend.

ngo shield; *synonyms* (*n*) screen, shelter, buffer, armor, protection, shade, defense, security, shell, covering, arms, casing, blind, (*v*) cover, guard, safeguard, preserve, secure, defend, hide, protect, buckler, harbor, patronize, keep, save, conceal, harbour, mask, cushion; *antonym* (*v*) expose.

ngobe eyelash; *synonyms* (*n*) cilium, lash, cut, eyewinker, hair, thong, whip, whiplash.

ngoma 1. spirit; *synonyms* (*n*) apparition, courage, ghost, life, mood, bravery, character, disposition, energy, enthusiasm, essence, heart, mind, phantom, soul, fortitude, dash, esprit, feeling, liveliness, mettle, pluck, shade, specter, sprite, morale, gist, pep, buoyancy, (*adj*) animation; *antonyms* (*n*) lethargy, body, **2**. evil spirit; *synonyms* (*n*) fiend, demon; **ruta ngoma** exercise.

ng'ombe cow; *synonyms* (*v*) bully, intimidate, awe, browbeat, daunt, terrorize, discourage, frighten, overawe, threaten, abash.

ngombo 1. slave; *synonyms* (*n*) serf, servant, bondman, inferior, thrall, bondsman, captive, vassal, dependent, (*v*) labor, drudge, fag, toil, work, moil, sweat, **2**. bond servant; *synonyms* (*n*) slave, bondslave, henchman.

ng'ondu sheep; *synonyms* (*n*) mutton, goat, cattle, follower, stock, antelopes, bison, bleater, camels, chevrotains, cloud, deer, giraffes, goats, livestock, oxen, prostitute, traditionalist, horses, pigs.

ngora cloth; *synonyms* (*n*) fabric, material, cover, rag, stuff, textile, calling, net, (*v*) napkin.

ngoro 1. spirit; *synonyms* (*n*) apparition, courage, ghost, life, mood, bravery, character, disposition, energy, enthusiasm, essence, heart, mind, phantom, soul, fortitude, dash, esprit, feeling, liveliness, mettle, pluck, shade, specter, sprite, morale, gist, pep, buoyancy, (*adj*) animation; *antonyms* (*n*) lethargy, body, **2.** soul; *synonyms* (*n*) man, creature, human, individual, person, personification, being, mortal, psyche, self, marrow, bosom, breast, embodiment, homo, someone, spirit, head, substance, somebody, (*adj*) core, quintessence, incarnation, backbone, genius, pith, quiddity, inspiration, lifeblood, sap, **3.** heart; *synonyms* (*n*) center, affection, basis, crux, hub, kernel, middle, guts, centre, fondness, nerve, nub, root, chest, boldness, base, intention, seat, content, focus, inside, interior, inwardness, meat, midst, nature, nucleus, pump, spunk, sum; *antonym* (*n*) edge.

ng'orota 1. snore; *synonyms* (*v*) snort, breathe, coma, doze, dream, hibernation, nap, siesta, snooze, (*n*) snoring, stertor, **2.** snort; *synonyms* (*n*) hoot, snicker, bird, boo, hiss, raspberry, razzing, sneer, snigger, (*v*) sniff, snore, huff, inhale, chuckle, giggle, titter.

ngu 1. clothes; *synonyms* (*n*) apparel, attire, clothing, dress, garb, garment, wardrobe, thing, gown, toggery, vesture, wear, **2.** material; *synonyms* (*n*) body, cloth, matter, stuff, fabric, substance, information, copy, element, equipment, (*adj*) bodily, corporal, corporeal, substantial, concrete, important, physical, real, essential, momentous, solid, tangible, actual, worldly, consequential, gross, earthly, relevant, secular, (*adv*) fleshly, **3.** firewood; *synonyms* (*n*) fuelwood, lumber, peat, petroleum, timber, turf, coal, energy, gas, oil, sticks.

nguhI short; *synonyms* (*adj*) brief, concise, scarce, brusque, close, curt, sharp, compendious, laconic, abrupt, deficient, diminutive, inadequate, insufficient, lacking, pithy, poor, scanty, small, blunt, scant, brittle, crisp, fleeting, gruff, light, little, (*adv*) abruptly, curtly, (*v*) compact; *antonyms* (*adj*) long, tall, high, lengthy.

ngui dog; *synonyms* (*n*) cur, andiron, blackguard, click, detent, cad, cock, heel, pawl, bounder, (*v*) chase, hound, beset, hunt, tail, track, trail, course, follow, persecute, pursue, shadow, tag, attend.

ngUkU 1. hen; *synonyms* (*n*) fowl, cock, chicken, biddy, rooster, poultry, mare, roe, sow, chick, partlet, capon, ruff, **2.** fowl; *synonyms* (*n*) bird, birds, birdie, boo, chickabiddy, dame, doll, ducks, game, geese, stock, wildfowl, hiss, hoot, pullet,

raspberry, razzing, shuttle, shuttlecock, skirt, snort, wench.

ngundi fist; *synonyms* (*n*) hand, grip, index, (*v*) finger, paw, neaf, neif, wrist.

ngunIko 1. cork; *synonyms* (*n*) bung, stopper, phellem, bob, bobber, bobfloat, (*v*) plug, cap, stop, close, (*adj*) cobweb, **2.** stopper; *synonyms* (*n*) stopple, top, closure, gate, (*v*) block, clog, obstruct.

ngUru 1. old; *synonyms* (*adj*) antiquated, obsolete, ancient, former, aged, antique, elderly, experienced, outdated, veteran, archaic, decrepit, hoary, mature, past, stale, disused, hackneyed, late, traditional, decayed, inveterate, auld, gray, musty, olden, older, outmoded, previous, primitive; *antonyms* (*adj*) new, young, modern, fresh, latest, novel, original, youthful, **2.** tortoise; *synonyms* (*n*) snail, testudo, (*v*) lingerer, loiterer, sluggard.

nguU hippopotamus; *synonyms* (*n*) hippo, pachyderm, zeekoe, rhinoceros, (*adj*) behemoth, cachalot, elephant, leviathan, porpoise, whale.

ngwaci sweet potato; *synonyms* (*n*) ocarina, bindweed.

nini small; *synonyms* (*adj*) little, minute, narrow, fine, inadequate, insignificant, low, minor, petty, slight, light, remote, cramped, young, limited, diminutive, faint, humble, miniature, minuscule, modest, paltry, short, slender, scanty, ungenerous, outside, poor, baby, feeble; *antonyms* (*adj*) bulky, colossal, considerable, enormous, extra-large, great, huge, sizeable, giant, major, (*syn*) big, large.

nja 1. outside; *synonyms* (*prep*) past, (*adj*) external, out, outdoor, foreign, extraneous, outer, away, outward, remote, slight, surface, distant, extrinsic, outlying, maximum, negligible, strange, top, international, largest, (*adv*) outdoors, alfresco, beyond, (*n*) exterior, periphery, outline; *antonyms* (*prep*) inside, in, (*adj*) indoor, internal, (*adv*) indoors, **2.** courtyard; *synonyms* (*n*) court, yard, area, square, backyard, forecourt.

njamba male; *synonyms* (*adj*) masculine, manly, virile, manful, manlike, (*n*) chap, guy, man, (*obj*) he; *antonyms* (*adj*) feminine, (*n*) female, woman.

njambe rooster; *synonyms* (*n*) chicken, cock, chanticleer, fowl, hen, partlet, poultry, prick.

njata star; *synonyms* (*n*) asterisk, celebrity, ace, principal, headliner, leading, luminary, personality, champion, idol, lead, world, bigwig, decoration, hero, hotshot, magnate, sensation, virtuoso, whiz, wizard, (*adj*) asteriated, (*v*) feature; *antonym* (*n*) nobody.

njau calf; *synonyms* (*n*) calfskin, sura, colt, foal, kitten, pup, shorthorn, kid, cow, doodle, dullard, foetus, loon, lout, lown, oaf, block, buzzard, freemartin, numps, put, stick, stock, yearling.

njege porcupine; *synonyms* (*n*) hedgehog, porpentine, shrew, (*adj*) beard, thistle.

njegeke armpit; *synonym* (*n*) axilla.

njeru 1. white; *synonyms* (*adj*) fair, ashen, blank, clean, snowy, wan, achromatic, bloodless, livid, pallid, colorless, bright, good, light, hoary, blanched, hot, milky, silver, (*n*) pale, whiteness, cornea, flannel, gabardine, iris, pupil, retina, tweed, (*v*) whiten, whitewash; *antonyms* (*adj*) dark, rosy, (*n*) black, **2.** new; *synonyms* (*adj*) green, modern, novel, original, additional, inexperienced, innovative, raw, recent, strange, unaccustomed, unprecedented, young, contemporary, current, different, newfangled, unfamiliar, unknown, virgin, extra, immature, modernistic, advanced, (*adv*) fresh, lately, freshly, recently, late, (*pron*) another; *antonyms* (*adj*) old, familiar, outgoing, second-hand, traditional, used, less, old-fashioned, stale, (*adv*) past.

njiarwo offspring; *synonyms* (*n*) issue, progeny, brood, children, family, child, descendant, descendants, lineage, posterity, race, seed, successor, young, consequence, scion, spawn, litter, materialization, (*v*) breed, fruit, generation, increase.

njIra highway; *synonyms* (*n*) road, highroad, way, course, path, route, street, thoroughfare.

njIthi 1. unripe; *synonyms* (*adj*) immature, green, raw, crude, premature, young, juvenile; *antonym* (*adj*) mature, **2.** uncooked; *synonyms* (*adj*) unblown, unpolished, tough, unfashioned, unformed, unhewn, unlabored, unwrought, pink, rare, red, underdone.

njogu elephant; *synonyms* (*n*) camel, dromedary, giant, llama, monster, (*adj*) behemoth, cachalot, whale, hippopotamus, leviathan, porpoise.

njohi beer; *synonyms* (*n*) cocktail, suds, bock, head, hops, lather, nip, oil, slops, snifter, soapsuds, stout, tipple, (*v*) wine, stingo, liqueur, spirits.

njora sword; *synonyms* (*n*) blade, rapier, brand, steel, glaive, knife, brond, firebrand, fox, intoxicate, make, mark, marque, morglay, point, stain, stigma, swerd, dirk, banger, baselard, beater, cimeter, claymore, dissension, dudgeon, kris, poniard, skean, stiletto.

njoru rotten; *synonyms* (*adj*) bad, foul, poor, fetid, lousy, musty, off, putrid, ill, shabby, corrupt, crappy, decomposed, sour, stinking, terrible, mean, vicious, low, decomposing, treacherous, atrocious, cheap, contemptible, despicable, dirty, (*v*) decayed, rancid, weak, effete; *antonym* (*adj*) fresh.

njoya fur; *synonyms* (*n*) coat, down, pelt, skin, fell, hair, fleece, feathers, fuzz, hide, nap, (*v*) blanket, flannel, (*adj*) pile, wool, floss.

njugI 1. fierce; *synonyms* (*adj*) bitter, violent, acute, cruel, ferocious, brutal, furious, grim, savage, nasty, angry, ardent, atrocious, barbarous, boisterous, fervent, fervid, intense, truculent, wicked, barbaric, fell, fiery, impetuous, keen, merciless, passionate, sharp, (*v*) vehement, wild; *antonyms* (*adj*) gentle, mild, **2.** sharp; *synonyms* (*adj*) intelligent, acid, acrid, harsh, incisive, penetrating, piercing, pointed, pungent, quick, severe, alert, caustic, cutting, piquant, prompt, sarcastic, smart, hot, astute, bright, discerning, distinct, high, lively, painful, (*v*) biting, brisk, clever, acrimonious; *antonyms* (*adj*) blunt, dull, rounded, sweet, bland, blurred, naive, round, smooth.

njuIrI hair; *synonyms* (*n*) fuzz, coat, down, fleece, fur, hairbreadth, haircloth, locks, pile, coiffure, (*adj*) brush, clipping, driblet.

njUkI bee; *synonyms* (*n*) honeybee, ant, termite, caprice, fancy, freak, humor, mania, mosquito, notion, party, phobia, whim, (*adj*) barbecue, (*v*) fly.

njUru bad; *synonyms* (*adj*) evil, adverse, harmful, immoral, naughty, poisonous, sad, sinister, wicked, malicious, infamous, appalling, awful, damaging, devilish, disagreeable, dreadful, hurtful, ill, mischievous, nasty, negative, off, putrid, rotten, sinful, sorry, stale, (*v*) decayed, rancid; *antonyms* (*adj*) fresh, pleasant, well, well-behaved, (*n*) good.

nnukuU corpse; *synonyms* (*n*) cadaver, carcass, body, corse, remains, stiff, clay.

noru fat; *synonyms* (*adj*) stout, corpulent, dense, thick, bulky, fatty, fertile, fleshy, gainful, greasy, great, gross, heavy, obese, overweight, plump, rich, stocky, big, ample, chubby, coarse, deep, dull, (*n*) avoirdupois, blubber, cream, (*v*) fatten, bloated, exaggerated; *antonyms* (*adj*) thin, slim, skinny, slender.

nU who; *synonyms* (*pron*) one, (*adj*) which, what.

nUgU 1. monk; *synonyms* (*n*) monastic, hermit, conventual, priest, cenobite, abbot, monkey, palmer, pilgrim, cleric, justice, minister, nun, parson, preacher, prior, recluse, rector, religieux, reverend, vicar, solitary, **2.** ape; *synonyms* (*n*) anthropoid, imitator, primate, chimpanzee, copycat, (*v*) mimic, mock, copy, echo, emulate, imitate, impersonate, caricature, counterfeit, simulate, parody, parrot, sham, **3.** baboon; *synonyms* (*n*) babion, oaf, langur, macaque, mangabey, patas, (*adj*) harridan, octopus, satyr, scarecrow, specter, toad.

nuguna 1. grumble; *synonyms* (*v*) murmur, mutter, complain, gripe, growl, rumble, grouch, mumble, roar, croak, gnarl, whine, carp, kick, maunder, scold, (*n*) complaint, moan, groan, roll, protest, wail, beef, grievance, grumbling, murmuring, rumbling, sound, thunder, **2.** grunt; *synonyms* (*n*) cry, (*v*) grumble, clamor.

nunga Uru smell; *synonyms* (*n*) odor, fragrance, savor, aroma, bouquet, odour, savour, stench, flavor, smack, feel, flavour, olfaction, relish, sense, breath, smelling, tang, trace, feeling, look, (*v*) reek, nose, perfume, scent, stink, sniff, snuff.

nunga wesa smell; *synonyms* (*n*) odor, fragrance, savor, aroma, bouquet, odour, savour, stench, flavor, smack, feel, flavour, olfaction, relish, sense, breath, smelling, tang, trace, feeling, look, (*v*) reek, nose, perfume, scent, stink, sniff, snuff.

nyaga ostrich; *synonyms* (*n*) estrich, (*adj*) antelope, chickaree, chipmunk, courser, doe, eagle, gazelle, greyhound, hackee, hare, squirrel, scorcher.

nyama meat; *synonyms* (*n*) flesh, core, essence, food, gist, heart, kernel, marrow, substance, crux, matter, beef, brawn, stuff, content, inwardness, nub, nucleus, pith, center, game, meaning, (*v*) grub, grubstake.

nyamu animal; *synonyms* (*n*) brute, creature, beast, organism, being, fauna, monster, (*adj*) bodily, carnal, brutal, corporeal, physical, sensual, primitive, (*adv*) fleshly; **nyamU yathI** serpent.

nyamU yathI 1. snake; *synonyms* (*n*) ophidian, serpent, hydra, (*v*) meander, wind, twist, coil, creep, curl, sneak, weave, **2.** serpent; *synonyms* (*n*) snake, viper, reptile, bassoon, contrafagotto, hautboy, oboe, (*v*) goose.

nyanya tomato; *synonyms* (*n*) cranberry, female, girl, prostitute, woman.

nyau cat; *synonyms* (*n*) caterpillar, guy, lynx, bozo, hombre, puss, barge, (*v*) disgorge, puke, regorge, regurgitate, retch, spew, spue, upchuck, vomit.

nyee testicle; *synonyms* (*n*) ball, testis, ballock, bollock, egg, nut, spermary, addict, baseball, chunk, clod, clump, crackpot, crank, eggs, en, freak, fruitcake, gem, glob, globe, gravestone, harden, insensibility, lump, mirror, nutcase, orb, orchis, screwball.

nyeki grass; *synonyms* (*n*) cannabis, forage, marijuana, pasture, dope, feed, ganja, herb, herbage, informer, lawn, marihuana, pasturage, weed, eatage, smoke, (*v*) betray, denounce, peach, rat, shit, snitch, (*adj*) pot, green, hemp.

nyiha diminish; *synonyms* (*v*) decrease, abate, decline, lessen, abridge, deduct, detract, dwindle, fall, reduce, depreciate, belittle, contract, curtail, retrench, shrink, alleviate, deflate, allay, cut, depress, fade, impair, lower, moderate, narrow, qualify, recede, relieve, (*adj*) degrade; *antonyms* (*v*) increase, grow.

nyingI 1. abundant; *synonyms* (*adj*) copious, generous, lush, luxuriant, thick, plenty, affluent, ample, fertile, fruitful, liberal, plentiful, prolific, rich, substantial, teeming, abounding, bountiful, considerable, enough, exuberant, full, fulsome, great, heavy, large, lavish, many, much, numerous; *antonyms* (*adj*) scarce, sparse, meager, **2.** many; *synonyms* (*adj*) manifold, abundant, countless, frequent, various, innumerable, multiple, several, different, numberless, (*n*) number; *antonym* (*n*) few.

nyitIro 1. haft; *synonyms* (*n*) handle, helve, hilt, heft, key, tiller, treadle, trigger, dwelling, **2.** handle;

synonyms (*v*) administer, conduct, feel, wield, control, deal, direct, finger, manage, manipulate, touch, treat, govern, cope, grope, ply, process, stock, work, apply, exercise, administrate, (*n*) grip, clutch, grasp, haft, handgrip, hold, knob, ear.

nyogonda twist; *synonyms* (*n*) twine, wind, spin, twirl, entwine, braid, kink, loop, strain, tangle, convolution, crook, (*v*) turn, bend, distort, curl, coil, contort, deform, curve, pervert, wrench, pull, roll, sprain, bias, entangle, intertwine, convolute, garble; *antonyms* (*v*) straighten, untwist.

nyongo bile; *synonyms* (*n*) anger, gall, ebullition, ferment, fume, pucker, fury, indignation, rage, malice, antipathy, bitterness, colera, dislike, hatred, offense, rancor, umbrage, warmth, boil, cheekiness, crust, freshness, impertinence, impudence, insolence, rancour.

nyoni bird; *synonyms* (*n*) birdie, chick, fowl, girl, wench, hiss, shuttlecock, insect, mollusk, reptile, shellfish, worm, person, biddy, boo, brid, clape, dame, doll, foul, hoot, mammal, missile, plane, raspberry, razzing, shuttle, skirt, (*v*) birdwatch, (*adj*) engaged.

nyota thirst; *synonyms* (*n*) desire, hunger, lust, longing, appetite, craving, dryness, hankering, yen, eagerness, thirstiness, yearning, envy, (*v*) crave, starve, wish, need, want.

nyotoka 1. quench; *synonyms* (*v*) extinguish, allay, appease, quash, destroy, assuage, slake, annihilate, calm, chill, cool, douse, fill, quell, satisfy, damp, choke, deaden, exterminate, quiet, satiate, slack, smother, squelch, stifle, subdue, suppress, blunt, cloy, (*n*) quenching, **2.** extinguish; *synonyms* (*v*) quench, eradicate, consume, end, devastate, crush, decimate, efface, eliminate, extirpate, obliterate, ravage, subvert, expunge, abolish, kill, raze, suffocate, terminate; *antonyms* (*v*) light, ignite.

nyua drink; *synonyms* (*n*) beverage, alcohol, brew, potion, swallow, crapulence, intoxicant, nip, potation, tipple, liquid, try, drinkable, drinking, drunkenness, (*v*) draught, booze, carouse, bib, absorb, down, gulp, pledge, swig, toast, bite, consume, eat, empty, (*adj*) dram.

nyumba house; *synonyms* (*n*) family, home, dwelling, firm, abode, domicile, building, edifice, habitation, housing, establishment, structure, ancestry, company, address, audience, business, concern, hall, household, mansion, place, race, residence, (*v*) accommodate, lodge, shelter, board, cover, (*adj*) descent.

nyUmU 1. dry; *synonyms* (*adj*) thirsty, arid, barren, boring, dehydrated, dull, bald, hoarse, jejune, plain, sober, tedious, cynical, exhausted, droughty, dreary, dusty, cold, baked, shriveled, fine, sapless, adust, empty, (*v*) dehydrate, desiccate, drain, uninteresting, sardonic, sear; *antonyms* (*adj*) wet, damp, moist, saturated, soaked, boggy, drenched, rainy, sodden, interesting, fresh, humid, juicy, succulent, sweaty, (v) drench, **2.** hard; *synonyms* (*adj*) austere, bad, difficult, grave, severe, strong, arduous, callous, cruel, grueling, knotty, tough, bitter, alcoholic, backbreaking, compact, complicated, dour, dry, forcible, grievous, rigid, rocky, rugged, thorny, (*adv*) firm, fast, firmly, (v) acute, (*n*) rough; *antonyms* (*adj*) easy, soft, kind, merciful, simple, soggy, tender, yielding, (*adv*) gently, lightly, **3.** dry land; *synonyms* (*n*) land, ground, country, acres, background, basis, commonwealth, demesne, domain, soil, estate, farming, footing, globe, kingdom, nation, primer, priming, realm, reason, state, undercoat, world.

nyUngU 1. vessel; *synonyms* (*n*) ship, boat, container, craft, duct, jar, vas, bowl, canal, pan, receptacle, basin, tube, watercraft, bottle, pipe, **2.** pot; *synonyms* (*n*) caldron, boiler, can, bucket, belly, cannabis, commode, flowerpot, grass, heap, jug, pile, pool, urn, kitty, pickle, ganja, hemp, marihuana, mess, potty, stomach, toilet, tub, (v) cure, plant, (*adj*) deal, marijuana, volume, hashish.

nyUrUrUka 1. glide; *synonyms* (*n*) slip, gliding, sailing, soaring, (v) slide, coast, float, flow, fly, run, drift, lapse, move, skid, slink, slither, soar, flit; *antonym* (v) struggle, **2.** trickle; *synonyms* (*n*) drip, distill, drivel, drool, (v) drop, dribble, percolate, leak, ooze, seep, filter, leach, bleed, drain, plash, pour, slobber, spirtle, splash, trill; *antonyms* (*n*) throng, (v) gush.

O

oha wrap up; *synonyms* (v) finish, envelop, wrap, cover, complete, finalize, enfold, terminate, close, conclude, consummate, determine, embrace, enclose, end, shroud, stop; *antonyms* (v) unwrap, start.

ona see; *synonyms* (v) look, feel, discover, appreciate, behold, consider, deem, discern, distinguish, know, notice, recognize, apprehend, ascertain, catch, envision, find, hear, inspect, learn, regard, witness, get, read, attend, call, check, comprehend, (*adj*) observe, perceive.

onania 1. produce; *synonyms* (v) give, effect, cause, make, bring, present, procreate, breed, construct, create, form, frame, generate, fetch, prepare, bear, beget, develop, do, engender, fabricate, get, grow, manufacture, originate, (*n*) gain, crop, invent, merchandise, proceeds, **2.** display; *synonyms* (*n*) array, presentation, appearance, screen, demonstration, exhibition, ostentation, scene, showing, spectacle, view, performance, fair, flash, manifestation, monitor, pageant, (v) exhibit, show, disclose, parade, expose, produce, brandish, flaunt,

indicate, reveal, demonstrate, discover, manifest; *antonym* (v) conceal.

onga suck; *synonyms* (v) draw, drink, imbibe, nurse, absorb, lactate, suckle, drain, puff, aspirate, pull, breastfeed, (*n*) sucking, suction.

ongerera increase; *synonyms* (*n*) gain, addition, augmentation, boom, expansion, extension, growth, progress, rise, accretion, development, enlargement, growing, improvement, (v) advance, accrue, extend, grow, aggrandize, expand, enhance, enlarge, deepen, accumulate, amplify, benefit, elevate, improve, propagate, (*adj*) augment; *antonyms* (*n*) reduction, contraction, decline, (v) decrease, reduce, diminish, drop, deteriorate.

ora rotten; *synonyms* (*adj*) bad, foul, poor, fetid, lousy, musty, off, putrid, ill, shabby, corrupt, crappy, decomposed, sour, stinking, terrible, mean, vicious, low, decomposing, treacherous, atrocious, cheap, contemptible, despicable, dirty, (v) decayed, rancid, weak, effete; *antonym* (*adj*) fresh.

ota bask; *synonyms* (v) lie, relax, enjoy, relish, revel, laze, doze, heat, loaf, lounge, savor, savour, wallow, indulge, insolate, loll, love, rollick, (*adj*) luxuriate, flush, glow, sweat, swelter, blaze, blister, boil, broil, burn, flame, reek.

oya 1. carry; *synonyms* (v) bear, bring, convey, conduct, take, acquit, behave, accept, comport, hold, pack, transport, load, assume, admit, adopt, act, capture, cart, channel, contain, deport, ferry, get, handle, haul, impress, keep, lug, move, **2.** take; *synonyms* (v) carry, catch, clutch, obtain, return, borrow, pick, acquire, appropriate, claim, demand, grab, have, interpret, require, select, steal, swallow, eat, devour, apply, choose, confiscate, consume, contract, direct, draw, elect, (*n*) seize, (*phr*) receive; *antonyms* (v) give, refuse, abstain, add, lose.

oyana igUrU 1. pick up; *synonyms* (v) arrest, get, acquire, learn, catch, collect, gather, lift, pick, receive, obtain, garner, cop, gain, grasp, hoist, improve, nab, raise, recover, recuperate, take, apprehend, hear, contract, extract, seize, attain, detain, (*n*) capture; *antonym* (v) put, **2.** lift up; *synonyms* (v) elevate, uplift, elate, intoxicate, collar, discover, glorify, inebriate, haul, nail, peck, percolate, perk, pull, see, soak.

R

rega refuse; *synonyms* (*v*) deny, reject, decline, disallow, dross, rebuff, disdain, dismiss, balk, dissent, defy, demur, disapprove, disavow, discard, repel, repudiate, resist, scorn, (*n*) garbage, trash, waste, offal, debris, litter, leavings, dirt, junk, recrement, rubbish; *antonym* (*v*) accept.

regana 1. refuse; *synonyms* (*v*) deny, reject, decline, disallow, dross, rebuff, disdain, dismiss, balk, dissent, defy, demur, disapprove, disavow, discard, repel, repudiate, resist, scorn, (*n*) garbage, trash, waste, offal, debris, litter, leavings, dirt, junk, recrement, rubbish; *antonym* (*v*) accept, **2.** reject; *synonyms* (*v*) refuse, eliminate, exclude, abandon, disown, ignore, renounce, spurn, eject, jettison, disclaim, discount, proscribe, reprobate, repulse, scrap, shun, despise, disbelieve, chuck, ditch, oppose, condemn, waive, avoid, except, override, abjure, contradict, (*n*) cull; *antonyms* (*v*) approve, choose, select, acknowledge, grant.

rehe 1. fetch; *synonyms* (*v*) carry, bring, convey, draw, elicit, attract, catch, get, retrieve, transport, conduct, extract, earn, bear, cause, transmit, acquire, arrest, arrive, come, make, obtain, produce, pull, take, transfer, (*n*) cheat, plant, trick, (*adj*) feint, **2.** bring; *synonyms* (*v*) fetch, put, reduce, afford, bestow, deliver, land, move, provide, beget, accompany, contribute, escort, hold, impart, institute, lead, lend, persuade, play, procure, work, wreak, add, convoy.

rIara finger; *synonyms* (*n*) digit, dactyl, (*v*) feel, handle, touch, hand, thumb, grope, indicate, paw, point, accuse.

rIga 1. leap; *synonyms* (*n*) bound, spring, vault, curvet, jumping, lunge, lope, bouncing, fault, leaping, saltation, boundary, bounds, confine, (*v*) jump, bounce, caper, dive, dance, hop, clear, pounce, skip, start, increase, ramp, buck, gambol, rear, rise; *antonyms* (*v*) fall, plummet, **2.** jump; *synonyms* (*v*) hurdle, startle, go, plunge, twitch, arise, raise, snatch, flip, grow, attack, bypass, climb, get, hike, move, shift, step, alternate, ambush, begin, derail, parachute, (*n*) leap, boost, lurch, drop, jolt, (*adj*) pretermit; *antonym* (*v*) decrease.

rIha pay; *synonyms* (*v*) compensate, compensation, liquidate, yield, afford, clear, expend, give, remunerate, indemnify, contribute, bear, hire, repay, requite, return, settle, grant, (*n*) recompense, wage, earnings, fee, salary, allowance, devote, income, remuneration, reward, make, charge; *antonym* (*v*) owe.

rIithia 1. look after; *synonyms* (*v*) keep, guard, attend, defend, maintain, protect, control, care, nurse, nurture, preserve, safeguard, save, tend, watch; *antonym* (*v*) neglect, **2.** care for; *synonyms* (*v*) cherish, fancy, like, love, treat, affect, raise.

rikia 1. complete; *synonyms* (*adj*) perfect, absolute, consummate, whole, full, stark, accomplished, all, finished, thorough, total, unabridged, utter, clean, comprehensive, (*v*) accomplish, achieve, close, finish, execute, act, attain, cease, clear, conclude, effect, fulfill, implement, perform, integrate; *antonyms* (*adj*) incomplete, partial, unfinished, abridged, shortened, sketchy, lacking, narrow, qualified, (*v*) neglect, **2.** finish; *synonyms* (*v*) end, complete, determine, discontinue, consume, do, stop, culminate, deplete, exhaust, expire, go, terminate, result, dispatch, drain, (*n*) conclusion, death, ending, finale, glaze, accomplishment, coating, completion, last, cessation, closing, coat, face, finis; *antonyms* (*v*) start, begin, continue, (*n*) beginning, **3.** do; *synonyms* (*v*) cheat, commit, conduct, make, practice, defraud, answer, arrange, build, cause, construct, play, serve, be, cut, behave, come, discharge, enact, fare, manage, operate, practise, (*n*) function, occasion, bash, deed, party, (*adj*) suffice, avail; *antonym* (*v*) unmake.

riko 1. kitchen; *synonyms* (*n*) cookroom, basement, offices, pantry, scullery, stomach, **2.** hearth; *synonyms* (*n*) fireplace, fire, fireside, chimney, furnace, home, abode, **3.** fireplace; *synonyms* (*n*) hearth, ingle, barbecue, blaze, favourite, flame, paramour, sweetheart.

ringa 1. knock; *synonyms* (*v*) hit, blow, bump, cuff, punch, strike, boot, clip, beat, condemn, criticize, knap, smack, thud, thump, wallop, carp, pelt, (*n*) rap, bang, tap, bash, crash, whack, clap, belt, clout, criticism, stroke, dint; *antonym* (*v*) praise, **2.** strike; *synonyms* (*n*) knock, assault, smash, attack, dab, pat, (*v*) impress, slap, move, affect, box, buffet, coin, collide, mint, touch, lash, hew, whip, afflict, clash, find, impact, pick, pound, reach, get, imprint, peck, (*adj*) play, **3.** cross; *synonyms* (*n*) crisscross, affliction, check, crossing, hybrid, mark, (*v*) intersect, baffle, cover, thwart, bilk, dash, divide, ford, meet, pass, (*adj*) crabbed, crabby, angry, cantankerous, grouchy, grumpy, traverse, cranky, annoyed, fractious, irritable, morose, peevish, perverse; *antonyms* (*v*) uncross, (*adj*) calm, good-tempered.

rIra 1. cry; *synonyms* (*n*) shout, bark, scream, yell, clamor, roar, bay, crying, buzz, exclamation, groan, hearsay, noise, report, rumor, sob, (*v*) call, bellow, shriek, weep, exclaim, howl, moan, outcry, screech, yelp, yowl, holler, hollo, squawk; *antonyms* (*v*) laugh, whisper, **2.** wail; *synonyms* (*n*) lament, complaint, lamentation, plaint, blast, yap, (*v*) cry, ululate, bawl, bewail, mewl, whimper, whine, squall, grieve, mourn, blubber, snivel, caterwaul, pule, waul, woof.

ririkana remember; *synonyms* (*v*) commemorate, recognize, recall, recollect, consider, record, remind, retain, think, review, ponder, mark, imagine, refresh, cite, memorialize, mention, reminisce, believe, commend, conceive, esteem, honor, intend, judge, mean, observe, retrospect; *antonym* (*v*) forget.

ritho eye; *synonyms* (*n*) optic, opinion, peeper, ring, sight, center, centre, oculus, (*v*) behold, see, view, gaze, stare, look, watch, glance, glimpse, examine, eyeball, regard.

ritU 1. serious; *synonyms* (*adj*) grave, heavy, sedate, austere, great, hard, considerable, critical, dangerous, earnest, grievous, sad, sober, bad, big, deep, major, severe, solemn, weighty, devout, acute, consequential, dull, grand, grim, pressing, (*v*) important, momentous, demure; *antonyms* (*adj*) frivolous, lighthearted, cheerful, flippant, humorous, mild, minor, playful, slight, **2.** heavy; *synonyms* (*adj*) dark, dense, fat, full, gross, arduous, bulky, burdensome, oppressive, thick, compact, ample, awkward, cumbersome, grueling, overweight, ponderous, sluggish, sound, strong, sullen, torpid, corpulent, fleshy, cloudy, languid, close, dreary, firm, (*n*) drowsy; *antonyms* (*adj*) light, easy, slim, thin, gentle, puny, skinny, **3.** dull; *synonyms* (*adj*) dim, blunt, bland, boring, cold, dismal, inactive, inert, obtuse, slack, slow, stupid, uninteresting, apathetic, commonplace, dingy, drab, flat, glassy, humdrum, lifeless, tame, tiresome, backward, hollow, bald, (*v*) deaden, dampen, damp, monotonous; *antonyms* (*adj*) bright, lively, sharp, exciting, interesting, lustrous, stimulating, amusing, exhilarating, glittery, glossy, glowing, high-pitched, intense, luminous, shiny, sparkling, varied, brisk, bubbly, clear, distinctive, imaginative, inspiring, risk-taking.

ritwa name; *synonyms* (*n*) call, title, epithet, address, appellation, denomination, designation, fame, mark, character, (*v*) appoint, baptize, describe, cite, designate, entitle, enumerate, identify, list, mention, constitute, denominate, itemize, make, nominate, quote, style, invoke, assign, commend.

roga bewitch; *synonyms* (*v*) fascinate, charm, enchant, attract, entrance, beguile, enamor, enrapture, spell, witch, influence, catch, conjure, enamour, enthrall, glamour, hex, lure, magnetize, mesmerize, ravish, spellbind, transport, becharm, (*n*) captivate, allure, entice, seduce, tempt, (*adj*) attach.

roho 1. spirit; *synonyms* (*n*) apparition, courage, ghost, life, mood, bravery, character, disposition, energy, enthusiasm, essence, heart, mind, phantom, soul, fortitude, dash, esprit, feeling, liveliness, mettle, pluck, shade, specter, sprite, morale, gist, pep, buoyancy, (*adj*) animation; *antonyms* (*n*) lethargy, body, **2.** soul; *synonyms* (*n*) man, creature, human, individual, person, personification, being, mortal, psyche, self, marrow, bosom, breast, embodiment, homo, someone, spirit, head, substance, somebody, (*adj*) core, quintessence, incarnation, backbone, genius, pith, quiddity, inspiration, lifeblood, sap.

rora 1. examine; *synonyms* (*v*) assay, audit, consider, overhaul, try, check, control, search, survey, ascertain, ask, contemplate, compare, analyze, canvass, essay, investigate, probe, quiz, review, study, test, view, appraise, collate, browse, analyse, discuss, explore, hear, **2.** glare; *synonyms* (*n*) blaze, brilliance, glance, scowl, shine, radiance, brightness, glow, lower, light, gaze, brilliancy, gleam, sheen, (*v*) beam, flame, flash, glower, frown, glitter, stare, flare, gape; *antonym* (*v*) smile, **3.** stare; *synonyms* (*v*) look, glare, peer, squint, goggle, see, watch, leer, (*n*) regard, **4.** look at; *synonyms* (*v*) deem, eye, examine, observe, inspect, notice, perceive, scan, deal, get.

rota dream; *synonyms* (*n*) daydream, aspiration, ambition, vision, desire, fantasy, figment, nightmare, reverie, sleep, coma, trance, notion, delusion, dreaming, phantom, conceit, (*v*) imagine, muse, contemplate, meditate, (*adj*) make-believe; *antonym* (*n*) reality.

ruambo peg; *synonyms* (*n*) bolt, pin, hook, dowel, leg, nog, stake, grade, tack, clothespin, remove, rowlock, scale, fling, join, link, oarlock, (*v*) nail, pitch, place, point, highball.

rUara groan; *synonyms* (*n*) grumble, cry, rumble, complaint, wail, gripe, screech, (*v*) moan, murmur, howl, mutter, sigh, complain, squeak, scrape, rasp, sough, mumble.

rUbaru rib; *synonyms* (*n*) ridge, vein, jest, wale, wife, button, peg, stay, (*v*) joke, tease, guy, mock, ridicule, helpmate, chaff, kid, blackguard.

rubiri dust; *synonyms* (*n*) powder, dirt, grit, relics, remains, rhino, soil, blunt, debris, defunct, detritus, grime, (*v*) clean, sprinkle, spray, wipe, spread, scatter, disperse, dot, mop.

rUbutu eyebrow; *synonyms* (*n*) brow, hair, supercilium, hilltop.

ruga cook; *synonyms* (*n*) chef, (*v*) boil, bake, brew, make, prepare, concoct, falsify, grill, poach, roast, simmer, stew, coddle, heat, do, fake, fix, fudge, hatch, manipulate, ready, wangle, alter, warm, (*adv*) color.

rugama pull up; *synonyms* (*v*) stop, uproot, halt, pull, raise, hike, hold; *antonym* (*v*) plant.

rUgendo journey; *synonyms* (*n*) jaunt, excursion, expedition, passage, trip, way, course, flight, outing, pilgrimage, tour, voyage, circuit, traverse, movement, route, exodus, journeying, progress, (*v*) go, travel, cruise, fare, navigate, ramble, ride, walk, hike, move, proceed.

rUgiri 1. enclosure; *synonyms* (*n*) coop, cage, barrier, enclosing, pen, hedge, addition, sty, case, envelopment, fencing, inclosure, insert, railing, ring, supplement, chamber, **2.** fence; *synonyms* (*n*) enclosure, hurdle, pale, bar, boundary, barricade, (*v*) wall, contend, enclose, parry, quibble, evade, palisade, surround, argue, box, compete, debate, envelop, equivocate.

ruheni lightning; *synonyms* (*n*) bolt, levin, bolter, dart, fetter, enlightenment, quarrel, shackle, (*v*) lightening, luminary, (*adj*) wind.

rUhI 1. hand; *synonyms* (*n*) deal, aid, applause, employee, paw, worker, support, assist, assistance, handwriting, help, indicator, mitt, needle, (*v*) deliver, give, pass, commit, bestow, afford, communicate, reach, grant, provide, devolve, line, gift, supply, feed, distribute, **2.** arm; *synonyms* (*n*) branch, wing, bay, department, division, limb, might, offshoot, power, section, sleeve, weapon, endow, member, (*v*) equip, furnish, outfit; *antonym* (*v*) disarm; **gUtha rUhi** slap.

rUhiU 1. scythe; *synonyms* (*n*) ankle, crane, crotch, crutch, elbow, fluke, groin, knee, knuckle, (*v*) sithe, **2.** sickle; *synonyms* (*n*) scythe, hook.

rUhonge branch; *synonyms* (*n*) arm, jump, wing, affiliate, ramus, member, division, limb, offshoot, outgrowth, section, shoot, stem, stick, subdivision, twig, group, area, realm, scion, stretch, chapter, class, department, domain, (*v*) fork, diverge, divide, split, (*adj*) tributary.

rUIgI kite; *synonyms* (*n*) parachute, airplane, epistle, former, letter, slip, (*v*) scram.

rUkobe eyelash; *synonyms* (*n*) cilium, lash, cut, eyewinker, hair, thong, whip, whiplash.

rUkUngU dust; *synonyms* (*n*) powder, dirt, grit, relics, remains, rhino, soil, blunt, debris, defunct, detritus, grime, (*v*) clean, sprinkle, spray, wipe, spread, scatter, disperse, dot, mop.

rUma 1. bite; *synonyms* (*n*) taste, bit, cheat, morsel, nibble, pain, sample, tang, spice, try, catch, chafe, chomp, food, juggle, piece, (*v*) sting, nip, chew, cut, pinch, burn, eat, erode, gnaw, hurt, munch, corrode, crunch, pierce, **2.** abuse; *synonyms* (*n*) affront, misuse, harm, outrage, reproach, invective, maltreatment, revilement, vilification, vituperation, attack, diatribe, blasphemy, (*v*) insult, mistreat, injure, assault, censure, damage, exploit, pervert, vilify, violate, vituperate, wrong, offense, rail, asperse, (*adj*) maltreat, profane; *antonyms* (*v*) praise, respect.

rUmanIrIra follow; *synonyms* (*v*) chase, pursue, adhere, adopt, accompany, comprehend, continue, ensue, grasp, hunt, realize, succeed, track, emulate, drive, fathom, absorb, arise, attend, be, come, comply, conform, do, fit, get, imitate, observe, (*adj*) catch, course; *antonyms* (*v*) precede, guide, head, lead.

rUmIrIra follow; *synonyms* (*v*) chase, pursue, adhere, adopt, accompany, comprehend, continue, ensue, grasp, hunt, realize, succeed, track, emulate, drive, fathom, absorb, arise, attend, be, come, comply, conform, do, fit, get, imitate, observe, (*adj*) catch, course; *antonyms* (*v*) precede, guide, head, lead.

rUmuru mosquito; *synonyms* (*n*) fly, alacran, alligator, crocodile, mugger, octopus, ant, bloodsucker, bug, insect, leech, musketo, parasite, tick, vermin, honeybee, vampire, (*v*) bee, wasp.

rungu 1. underneath; *synonyms* (*prep*) below, under, (*adv*) beneath, (*n*) bottom, (*adj*) down, inferior, **2.** below; *synonyms* (*adv*) infra, downstairs, (*prep*) underneath, (*adj*) low, after; *antonyms* (*prep*) above, over.

rurigi string; *synonyms* (*n*) chain, file, row, strand, twine, range, cord, filament, rank, series, thread, tie, sequence, fiber, procession, rope, train, wire, yarn, drawstring, concatenation, ribbon, strip, succession, (*v*) run, hang, chord, draw, fasten, (*adj*) line.

rUrImI tongue; *synonyms* (*n*) language, dialect, idiom, lingua, speech, clapper, glossa, talk, knife, lingo, palate, parlance, spit, vernacular, (*v*) lick, (*adj*) flippancy, flowing, fluency.

ruta 1. do; *synonyms* (*v*) act, cheat, commit, accomplish, complete, conduct, perform, achieve, make, practice, defraud, answer, arrange, build, cause, construct, execute, play, serve, be, cut, behave, come, discharge, (*n*) function, occasion, bash, deed, (*adj*) suffice, avail; *antonyms* (*v*) neglect, unmake, **2.** take off; *synonyms* (*v*) deduct, leave, mock, go, remove, ape, copy, depart, fly, imitate, impersonate, mimic, quit, soar, subtract, abscond, ascend, begin, doff, flee, move, part, reduce, rise, scram, start; **ruta ngoma** exercise.

ruta ngoma exercise; *synonyms* (*n*) practice, employment, application, discipline, play, movement, action, activity, example, function, operation, rehearsal, work, maneuver, assignment, (*v*) drill, apply, employ, use, exert, train, educate, do, utilize, wield, behave, habituate, accustom, act, execute.

rutana 1. teach; *synonyms* (*v*) inform, enlighten, coach, educate, instruct, indoctrinate, drill, learn, lecture, school, direct, discipline, form, tell, train, tutor, catechize, edify, demonstrate, apprise, develop, discover, ground, improve, inculcate, prepare, (*adj*) guide, show, **2.** instruct; *synonyms* (*v*) charge, advise, teach, command, bid, enjoin, ~~admonish, brief, communicate, breed,~~ apprize, dictate, order, initiate, conduct, counsel, acquaint, commission, lesson, lead, manage, nourish, nurture, rear, require, warn, cultivate, encourage, enforce, illuminate; *antonym* (*v*) request.

rutanja put out; *synonyms* (*v*) issue, douse, extend, extinguish, publish, quench, bother, inconvenience, irritate, disturb, release, disappoint, discommode, disoblige, trouble, annoy, smother, vex, anaesthetize, anesthetize, disconcerted, displease, dowse, eliminate, (*adj*) upset, dissatisfied, discontented, disgruntled, hurt, (*n*) dissatisfy; *antonym* (*adj*) pleased.

rUtha 1. permission; *synonyms* (*n*) consent, license, permit, approval, authority, leave, liberty, licence, agreement, assent, authorization, dispensation, pass, sanction, approbation, concession, acquiescence, endorsement, dismissal, admission, accord, blessing, concurrence, right, sufferance, warrant, entry, (*v*) allowance, allow, grant; *antonym* (*n*) refusal, **2.** leave; *synonyms* (*v*) depart, forsake, go, abandon, desert, quit, escape, flee, lead, lay, bequeath, drop, evacuate, let, relinquish, start, rest, abdicate, discharge, afford, commit, ditch, dump, entrust, (*n*) furlough, holiday, permission, break, part, (*adj*) empty; *antonyms* (*v*) arrive, enter, stay, remain, approach, change, come.

rUthingo wall; *synonyms* (*n*) partition, bar, barrier, bulwark, rampart, cliff, earthwork, fortification, screen, rail, barricade, block, blockade, bolt, breakwater, divider, embankment, groyne, hurdle, impediment, lock, obstruction, padlock, paries, parietes, wainscot, (*v*) fence, palisade, surround.

rUthuthuU drizzle; *synonyms* (*n*) rainfall, wet, (*v*) mizzle, rain, mist, spray, drip; *antonym* (*v*) pour.

rwara 1. sick; *synonyms* (*adj*) ill, queasy, ailing, indisposed, poorly, weary, invalid, diseased, morbid, sickly, nauseous, poor, crazy, disgusted, nauseated, upset, perverted, distressed, bad, disordered, frail, pale, (*n*) infirm, (*v*) unwell, puke, vomit, heave, disgorge, regurgitate, spew; *antonyms* (*adj*) well, healthy, **2.** fingernail; *synonym* (*n*) claw.

rwImbo song; *synonyms* (*n*) melody, air, strain, cry, warble, poem, tune, call, chanson, canticle, poetry, rhyme, verse, birdcall, birdsong, chorus, composition, release, (*v*) ditty, chant, sing, (*adj*) lay, ballad.

T

tahika vomit; *synonyms* (*n*) regurgitation, vomiting, emetic, emesis, vomitus, disgorgement, nauseant, puking, (*v*) spew, heave, puke, cast, disgorge, retch, sick, gag, eject, barf, cat, chuck, regorge, regurgitate, spue, upchuck, honk, parbreak.

tamUka pronounce; *synonyms* (*v*) enunciate, articulate, affirm, declare, say, assert, deliver, express, utter, announce, decree, judge, proclaim, rule, speak, vocalize, pass, adjudicate, enounce, state, voice, prolate, aver, comment, (*n*) allege, give, maintain, adjudge, contend, (*adj*) discharge.

taranIria add up; *synonyms* (*v*) add, total, aggregate, amount, sum, tally, tot, come, number.

tarIria explain; *synonyms* (*v*) comment, elucidate, interpret, account, clarify, decipher, define, describe, enlighten, excuse, explicate, expound, gloss, solve, denote, annotate, answer, demonstrate, expand, illuminate, illustrate, read, resolve, reveal, show, unfold, develop, clear, disclose, understand; *antonym* (*v*) confuse.

tata aunt; *synonyms* (*n*) auntie, aunty, uncle, nephew, niece.

tawa lamp; *synonyms* (*n*) light, look, beacon, view, glance, alfalfa, glimpse, lucern, generator, (*v*) behold, regard, perceive, gape, gaze, inspect, observe, recognize.

tega fish; *synonyms* (*n*) bird, insect, mollusk, shellfish, worm, amphibian, beginner, blacktail, cob, cobnut, corkwing, dart, defense, dollar, dracunculus, dupe, excuse, (*v*) angle, seek, hunt, pursue, grope, rummage, beg, chowder, chupatty, clam, compote, damper, (*adj*) frail.

tegura 1. remove; *synonyms* (*v*) oust, take, pull, eject, expel, deduct, discharge, strip, delete, erase, evacuate, extract, abolish, get, dislodge, draw, empty, eliminate, eradicate, exclude, move, transport, withdraw, banish, carry, doff, dismantle, (*n*) displace, (*adj*) clear, free; *antonyms* (*v*) insert, install, place, **2.** wave; *synonyms* (*n*) billow, gesture, motion, sign, surge, signal, breaker, vibration, nod, rash, tide, undulation, (*v*) brandish, flap, flutter, curl, flourish, swell, swing, undulate, beat, beckon, ripple, shake, sway, oscillate, roll, kink, fluctuate, gesticulate.

tene old times; *synonyms* (*n*) langsyne, age, antiquity, past.

teng'era run; *synonyms* (*v*) flow, rule, dash, gush, race, career, conduct, direct, function, go, hasten, hurry, operate, pour, progress, rush, dribble, walk, administer, bleed, channel, control, (*n*) pass, campaign, course, drive, range, sequence, tide, (*adj*) stream.

thaburia 1. vessel; *synonyms* (*n*) ship, boat, container, craft, duct, jar, vas, bowl, canal, pan, receptacle, basin, tube, watercraft, bottle, pipe, **2.** pot; *synonyms* (*n*) caldron, boiler, can, bucket, belly, cannabis, commode, flowerpot, grass, heap, jug, pile, pool, urn, kitty, pickle, ganja, hemp, marihuana, mess, potty, stomach, toilet, tub, (*v*) cure, plant, (*adj*) deal, marijuana, volume, hashish.

thagi buttermilk; *synonym* (*n*) milk.

thaka beautiful; *synonyms* (*adj*) attractive, good-looking, bright, beauteous, fine, handsome, lovely, picturesque, pleasant, pretty, striking, sweet, adorned, ornate, dainty, stylish, bonny, charming, cute, delightful, divine, elegant, exquisite, fair, glorious, graceful, heavenly, refined, splendid, tasteful; *antonyms* (*adj*) ugly, unattractive.

thakame blood; *synonyms* (*n*) ancestry, birth, gore, descent, family, kindred, lineage, origin, beau, bloodshed, consanguinity, coxcomb, exquisite, extraction, line, murder, parentage, pedigree, relationship, stock, strain, blade, rank, (*adj*) humor, juice, lymph, sap.

thama migrate; *synonyms* (*v*) immigrate, emigrate, move, transmigrate, flit, travel, depart, fleet, flutter, leave, scatter, drift, journey, nomadize, rove, voyage.

thambia wash; *synonyms* (*v*) rinse, paint, bathe, clean, lave, moisten, mop, scour, scrub, color, tint, lap, gargle, dampen, launder, splash, wet, dye, swill, (*n*) soak, ablution, washing, swamp, bath, laundry, lotion, marsh, swash, tinge, coat; *antonym* (*v*) dirty.

thandI spark; *synonyms* (*n*) flicker, light, glimmer, arc, blaze, fire, flame, scintilla, scintillation, shimmer, trace, discharge, gaillard, jester, joker, luminosity, (*v*) flash, sparkle, gleam, glint, glitter, activate, glisten, trigger, stir, twinkle, actuate.

thata barren; *synonyms* (*adj*) infertile, sterile, deserted, abortive, arid, dry, fruitless, meagre, stark, void, bleak, dead, desert, desolate, devoid, effete, idle, meager, poor, unfruitful, unproductive, vain, acarpous, bald, impotent, null, purposeless, (*v*) bare, lean, (*n*) waste; *antonyms* (*adj*) fertile, lush, productive.

thathi broth; *synonyms* (*n*) liquor, consommé, puree, stock, brew, (*v*) potage, pottage, beverage.

theerI monk; *synonyms* (*n*) monastic, hermit, conventual, priest, cenobite, abbot, monkey, palmer, pilgrim, cleric, justice, minister, nun, parson, preacher, prior, recluse, rector, religieux, reverend, vicar, solitary.

theka laugh; *synonyms* (*n*) chuckle, chortle, jest, gag, jape, laughter, cackle, sneer, scream, jeer, caper, snigger, snort, (*v*) joke, giggle, smile, titter, snicker, beam; *antonym* (*v*) cry.

thigino sweat; *synonyms* (*n*) labor, perspiration, lather, sudor, effort, struggle, drudgery, fret, labour, stew, exertion, diaphoresis, hidrosis, trouble, slog, travail, endeavor, (*v*) work, perspire, toil, drudge, exude, ooze, moil, strain, strive, (*adj*) glow.

thiI 1. go; *synonyms* (*v*) come, elapse, pass, break, crack, depart, disappear, drive, run, travel, fall, extend, function, operate, ride, turn, work, arrive, blow, course, pace, act, belong, decease, die, (*n*) fare, attempt, effort, (*adj*) follow, move, 2. go away; *synonyms* (*v*) leave, exit, go, separate, vacate, vanish, (*int*) away; *antonym* (*v*) stay, 3. leave; *synonyms* (*v*) forsake, abandon, desert, quit, escape, flee, lead, lay, allow, bequeath, drop, evacuate, let, relinquish, start, rest, abdicate, discharge, afford, (*n*) furlough, holiday, permission, permit, consent, liberty, license, part, authorization, allowance, (*adj*) empty; *antonyms* (*v*) enter, remain, approach, change, 4. go out; *synonyms* (*v*) date, ebb, expire, ascertain, assure, attend, catch, check,

consider, construe, control, determine, discover, draw, encounter, ensure, entrust, envision, escort, examine, experience, fancy, figure, find, forget, give, see, socialize, (*int*) out, begone.

thIinI inside; *synonyms* (*adv*) indoors, inwardly, within, (*n*) interior, middle, center, stomach, bosom, contents, (*adj*) inner, internal, indoor, inland, inward, private, privileged; *antonyms* (*prep*) outside, (*n*) exterior, (*adj*) free; **ingIra thIini** penetrate.

thika bury; *synonyms* (*v*) immerse, inter, overwhelm, cloak, conceal, entomb, hide, mask, secrete, cache, cover, embed, engulf, forget, inhume, intomb, plant, screen, sepulchre, sink, swallow, tomb, (*n*) grave; *antonyms* (*v*) exhume, unearth.

thikIrIria listen; *synonyms* (*v*) hark, hear, attend, hearken, heed, harken, list, mind, concentrate, incline.

thima 1. examine; *synonyms* (*v*) assay, audit, consider, overhaul, try, check, control, search, survey, ascertain, ask, contemplate, compare, analyze, canvass, essay, investigate, probe, quiz, review, study, test, view, appraise, collate, browse, analyse, discuss, explore, hear, 2. measure; *synonyms* (*n*) amount, criterion, extent, beat, benchmark, degree, estimate, measurement, meter, quantity, act, allotment, action, bill, dose, magnitude, pace, portion, proceeding, rate, scale, time, bulk, (*v*) grade, assess, evaluate, fathom, gauge, value, (*adj*) mete, 3. test; *synonyms* (*n*) trial, audition, experiment, examination, measure, inspection, endeavor, exam, experience, experimentation, tryout, ordeal, analysis, scrutiny, effort, testing, (*v*) examine, prove, sample, attempt, proof, verify, screen, taste, feel, tempt, see, sound, (*adj*) experimental, pilot.

thIna 1. distress; *synonyms* (*n*) agony, anguish, pain, trouble, anxiety, calamity, difficulty, grief, hurt, torture, adversity, affliction, alarm, misery, sorrow, suffering, disquiet, destitution, ache, shock, (*v*) afflict, torment, concern, bother, upset, worry, discomfort, annoy, distraint, ail; *antonyms* (*v*) comfort, please, 2. hardship; *synonyms* (*n*) distress, grievance, burden, disaster, asperity, deprivation, misfortune, poverty, trial, catastrophe, hardness, strait, neediness, penury, pressure, rigour, severity, want, grimness, rigor; *antonym* (*n*) affluence.

thIni inside; *synonyms* (*adv*) indoors, inwardly, within, (*n*) interior, middle, center, stomach, bosom, contents, (*adj*) inner, internal, indoor, inland, inward, private, privileged; *antonyms* (*prep*) outside, (*n*) exterior, (*adj*) free.

thinja slaughter; *synonyms* (*n*) massacre, carnage, bloodshed, butchery, drubbing, homicide, killing, thrashing, destruction, beating, butchering, annihilation, slaying, walloping, whipping, debacle, trouncing, (*v*) murder, butcher, defeat, assassinate, kill, slay, exterminate, gore, destroy, execute, annihilate, thrash, trounce.

thitUra 1. jerk; *synonyms* (*n*) tug, heave, pull, fool, dork, jog, idiot, (*v*) jolt, jump, shake, yank, jar, twitch, fling, bump, flip, bob, bounce, convulse, draw, flick, hitch, recoil, start, buck, cast, chuck, agitate, flinch, haul, **2.** startle; *synonyms* (*v*) alarm, frighten, scare, astonish, shock, astound, amaze, dismay, electrify, rouse, stagger, terrify, disturb, panic, appall, daunt, dumbfound, stun, fluster, galvanize, originate, perturb, ruffle, (*n*) leap, (*adv*) surprise.

thoma read; *synonyms* (*v*) interpret, construe, decipher, gather, indicate, learn, perceive, say, understand, demonstrate, comprehend, display, examine, explain, peruse, record, register, scan, show, study, take, translate, ascertain, check, decode, hear, declare, foretell, infer, look.

thombocania mix; *synonyms* (*n*) mixture, concoction, combination, miscellany, admixture, assortment, (*v*) alloy, blend, intermingle, mingle, combine, compound, confound, intermix, join, meld, merge, aggregate, admix, immingle, associate, coalesce, confuse, consort, fuse, immix, incorporate, jumble, amalgamate, commingle; *antonym* (*v*) separate.

thondeka 1. put right; *synonyms* (*v*) rectify, repair, amend, right, mend, fix, remedy, **2.** prepare; *synonyms* (*v*) arrange, form, plan, dress, coach, devise, lay, make, set, adjust, concoct, cook, equip, fit, groom, organize, qualify, discipline, contrive, condition, do, mount, compose, exercise, provide, train, adapt, cultivate, (*n*) design, (*adj*) prime, **3.** repair; *synonyms* (*n*) overhaul, renewal, renovation, fixing, mending, reparation, restoration, upkeep, (*v*) patch, redress, correct, cure, compensate, doctor, renovate, restore, heal, go, reclaim, recover, renew, resort, reform, redeem, refresh, reinstate, bushel, reconstruct, retrieve, haunt; *antonym* (*v*) break, **4.** arrange; *synonyms* (*v*) appoint, order, settle, pack, agree, classify, decorate, engineer, put, reconcile, straighten, display, align, dispose, distribute, file, group, manage, marshal, place, position, prepare, range, regulate, sort, tabulate, heap, stand, edit, (*n*) array; *antonyms* (*v*) disturb, disarrange, **5.** construct; *synonyms* (*v*) build, erect, fabricate, constitute, manufacture, produce, raise, rear, assemble, compile, create, fashion, shape, fabric, cause, craft, establish, forge, found, frame, generate, invent, model, originate, perform, (*n*) concept, conception, notion, idea, thought; *antonyms* (*v*) destroy, demolish, **6.** put together; *synonyms* (*v*) combine, construct, join, weave, incorporate, mix, configure, connect, edify, piece, (*adv*) collectively, conjointly, jointly.

thondekania arrange; *synonyms* (*v*) adjust, appoint, dress, order, set, settle, pack, adapt, agree, classify, compose, decorate, do, engineer, fix, provide, put,

reconcile, straighten, display, align, design, dispose, distribute, file, form, group, manage, marshal, (*n*) array; *antonyms* (*v*) disturb, disarrange.

thoni 1. modesty; *synonyms* (*n*) chastity, decency, reserve, bashfulness, humility, diffidence, humbleness, coyness, gentleness, continence, reservation, honor, simplicity, propriety, shyness, virtue, (*adj*) honesty; *antonyms* (*n*) arrogance, pretentiousness, self-importance, immodesty, spectacle, **2.** shame; *synonyms* (*n*) reproach, disgrace, discredit, humiliation, chagrin, insult, modesty, pity, scandal, contempt, degradation, embarrassment, humble, ignominy, infamy, mortification, opprobrium, odium, guilt, disrepute, (*v*) dishonor, degrade, humiliate, abash, debase, confuse, embarrass, discountenance, attaint, dishonour, **3.** disgrace; *synonyms* (*n*) shame, blemish, stain, slur, abuse, taint, defect, obloquy, stigma, blur, disregard, disrespect, disparagement, fault, flaw, outrage, slander, smear, baseness, (*v*) blot, defame, defile, demean, spot, abase, mortify, lower, soil, tarnish, (*adj*) ashame; *antonyms* (*v*) respect, credit, esteem.

thuguma urinate; *synonyms* (*v*) pee, piddle, micturate, piss, excrete, make, urine, addle, attain, build, cause, clear, constitute, construct, cook, crap, create, defecate, do, draw, earn, establish, fix, form, gain, get, give, have, hit, hold.

thUka rotten; *synonyms* (*adj*) bad, foul, poor, fetid, lousy, musty, off, putrid, ill, shabby, corrupt, crappy, decomposed, sour, stinking, terrible, mean, vicious, low, decomposing, treacherous, atrocious, cheap, contemptible, despicable, dirty, (*v*) decayed, rancid, weak, effete; *antonym* (*adj*) fresh.

thUkia 1. destroy; *synonyms* (*v*) break, demolish, blight, despoil, annihilate, blast, crush, dash, destruct, devastate, devour, dismantle, end, eradicate, extinguish, kill, raze, slay, spoil, subvert, waste, wreck, crash, batter, damage, (*adj*) desolate, abolish, consume, cancel, (*n*) murder; *antonyms* (*v*) build, preserve, create, make, **2.** spoil; *synonyms* (*v*) plunder, corrupt, impair, rot, deface, indulge, injure, mar, sack, baby, botch, bungle, coddle, deprave, disfigure, frustrate, hurt, pamper, pillage, ravage, ransack, blemish, contaminate, cosset, decay, defile, (*n*) ruin, prey, booty, (*adj*) harm; *antonyms* (*v*) enhance, improve, conserve, **3.** blind; *synonyms* (*adj*) sightless, undiscerning, dark, eyeless, thoughtless, unreasoning, involuntary, (*v*) bedazzle, daze, dazzle, obscure, dim, automatic, (*n*) screen, curtain, shutter, awning, drape, trick, veil, camouflage, cheat, cloak, concealment, cover, deceit, front, mask, subterfuge, sunshade; *antonym* (*adj*) sighted.

thUko rotten; *synonyms* (*adj*) bad, foul, poor, fetid, lousy, musty, off, putrid, ill, shabby, corrupt, crappy, decomposed, sour, stinking, terrible, mean, vicious, low, decomposing, treacherous, atrocious, cheap, contemptible, despicable, dirty, (v) decayed, rancid, weak, effete; antonym (adj) fresh.

thumu mature; synonyms (adj) ripe, complete, adult, aged, developed, experienced, fledged, old, perfect, due, prime, big, finished, matured, payable, whole, advanced, sophisticated, (v) grow, ripen, develop, age, maturate, mellow, season, digest, elaborate, become, evolve, fructify; antonyms (adj) childish, naive, unripe, young, sophomoric, (v) immature.

thUngi bladder; synonyms (n) cyst, vesica, balloon, capsule, utricle, vesicle, calyx, cancelli, newspaper, pod, (v) inflate.

thura 1. set up; synonyms (v) build, erect, raise, establish, found, assemble, construct, institute, mount, rear, arrange, create, fix, frame, install, introduce, organize, pitch, prepare, entrap, devise, elevate, launch, order, set, ready, organise, constitute, base, develop; antonym (v) disband, **2.** appoint; synonyms (v) assign, nominate, accredit, delegate, designate, prescribe, choose, commission, depute, destine, elect, make, ordain, hire, allot, attach, allocate, call, charge, command, consign, detail, employ, equip, furnish, outfit, place, point, select, (n) name.

thutha back; synonyms (adv) before, backward, (n) rear, reverse, spine, (adj) assist, posterior, (v) support, advocate, endorse, recede, second, stake, vouch, guarantee, aid, champion, encourage, finance, fund, gamble, help, promote, sanction, sponsor, sustain, uphold, warrant, approve, defend; antonyms (n) face, (v) front, oppose, advance.

thuura choose; synonyms (v) adopt, elect, pick, prefer, select, appoint, take, assign, decide, desire, determine, draw, excerpt, like, vote, wish, nominate, designate, resolve, please, extract, buy, fancy, gather, collect, covet, cull, love, opt, want; antonyms (v) reject, refuse.

tia honor; synonyms (n) award, fame, glory, reputation, accolade, compliment, reverence, reward, deference, celebrity, credit, estimation, homage, favor, name, honesty, honour, (v) esteem, respect, celebrate, grace, worship, glorify, dignify, adore, distinguish, praise, (adj) chastity, dignity, renown; antonyms (n) shame, humiliation, (v) dishonor, disgrace, break, ignore.

tiga leave; synonyms (v) depart, forsake, go, abandon, desert, quit, escape, flee, lead, lay, allow, bequeath, drop, evacuate, let, relinquish, start, rest, abdicate, (n) furlough, holiday, permission, permit, break, consent, liberty, license, part, authorization, (adj) empty; antonyms (v) arrive, enter, stay, remain, approach, change, come.

tigwo stay; synonyms (v) remain, reside, rest, prop, stop, abide, continue, endure, pause, arrest, bide, dwell, support, linger, lodge, persist, sojourn, stand, wait, interrupt, (n) delay, halt, check,

postponement, reprieve, respite, abode, (adj) cease, inhabit, tarry; antonyms (v) leave, change, abscond, depart.

tIIri 1. soil; synonyms (n) ground, dirt, grime, land, dust, tarnish, region, sand, clod, (v) smudge, blot, contaminate, dirty, pollute, mire, blemish, defile, foul, mould, smear, smirch, smutch, begrime, daub, stain, sully, bedaub, bemire, (adj) blur, filth; antonym (v) clean, **2.** sand; synonyms (n) grit, guts, beach, coast, seaside, backbone, gumption, shore, (v) sandpaper, rub, smooth, (adj) powder.

tinia 1. slash; synonyms (n) cut, gash, rip, slice, split, cleft, diagonal, scratch, blaze, (v) reduce, hack, clip, hew, tear, wound, fell, chop, flog, lash, slit, whip, pare, strike, abridge, decrease, crop, drop, slam, carve, curtail, **2.** cut; synonyms (v) abbreviate, bite, condense, fashion, shorten, snub, trim, cleave, dilute, edit, hurt, ignore, lower, sever, shave, slight, thin, (n) notch, cutting, nick, blow, shape, slash, clipping, break, crack, form, rift, section, share; antonyms (v) increase, lengthen, (n) addition, extension.

tombo brain; synonyms (n) mastermind, genius, head, mind, reason, brainpower, brains, encephalon, intelligence, mentality, nous, psyche, wit, prodigy.

tonyerera sink; synonyms (n) sag, basin, (v) decline, dip, droop, fall, set, descend, drop, fell, bury, collapse, decay, flag, founder, lower, settle, subside, ebb, languish, abate, decrease, die, plunge, fade, disappear, degenerate, deteriorate, (adj) immerse, bog; antonyms (v) rise, float.

toro sleep; synonyms (n) nap, doze, kip, slumber, lie, dream, siesta, quietus, relaxation, remainder, residue, stupor, (v) rest, repose, catnap, hibernate, nod, lodge, snooze, quiet, couch, perch, recline, settle, (adj) abide; **koma toro** sleep.

tua mata spit; synonyms (n) broach, saliva, cape, expectoration, spittle, spitting, image, (v) drizzle, impale, expectorate, skewer, spew, sprinkle, drool, spike, hiss, spatter, disgorge, gore, hawk, transfix, splutter, enfilade, patter, ptyalize, spear.

tukania 1. put together; synonyms (v) erect, assemble, build, combine, construct, join, prepare, create, fabricate, form, organize, frame, make, produce, arrange, compose, weave, compile, incorporate, mix, raise, configure, connect, edify, manufacture, piece, place, (adv) collectively, conjointly, jointly, **2.** mix; synonyms (n) mixture, concoction, combination, miscellany, admixture, assortment, commixture, (v) alloy, blend, intermingle, mingle, compound, confound, intermix, meld, merge, aggregate, admix, immingle, associate, coalesce, confuse, consort, fuse, immix, jumble, amalgamate, commingle, commix, integrate; antonym (v) separate.

tuma 1. weave; synonyms (v) twine, twist, braid, knit, entwine, interweave, wind, waver, plait, fabricate, tissue, lurch, interlace, reel, join, intertwine, meander, sway, thread, totter, wobble, (*n*) texture, wander, **2.** sew; *synonyms* (*v*) patch, mend, stitch, tack, tailor, retick, tick, weave, make, beat, click, create, customise, customize, cut, fasten, hoist, raise, repair, bind, detail, (*n*) delicacy, (*adj*) tie, pinion, strap, string, bandage, buckle, button, chain, **3.** send; *synonyms* (*v*) despatch, pass, convey, deliver, dispatch, forward, give, mail, post, carry, divert, project, beam, cast, channel, commit, consign, direct, place, put, throw, transmit, transport, discharge, fling, conduct, propel, air, broadcast, charge, **4.** knit; *synonyms* (*v*) pucker, bond, purse, crease, interconnect, interlink, knot, link, net, splice, cockle, crumple, heal, (*n*) knitting, knitwork, (*adj*) lace.

tUnga meet; *synonyms* (*v*) converge, find, assemble, congregate, encounter, fulfill, gather, answer, cross, confront, intersect, abut, concur, adjoin, collect, convene, face, join, satisfy, catch, correspond, discharge, fill, fulfil, get, perform, (*n*) match, meeting, (*adj*) fit, fitting; *antonyms* (*v*) avoid, disperse, diverge.

turia ndu kneel; *synonyms* (*v*) bow, cringe, bob, dip, duck, stoop, crouch, fawn, grovel, kowtow, curtsey, (*n*) kneeling, tolling.

U

ucUrU gruel; *synonym* (*n*) loblolly.

Ugo magic; *synonyms* (*adj*) magical, charming, supernatural, occult, sorcerous, witching, wizard, wizardly, mystic, (*n*) conjuration, incantation, charm, enchantment, legerdemain, sorcery, glamour, fascination, illusion, theurgy, trick, deception, attraction, artifice, magnetism, spell, thaumaturgy, wizardry.

UgUta 1. sloth; *synonyms* (*n*) laziness, idleness, indolence, lethargy, acedia, inactivity, inaction, inertia, listlessness, slothfulness, **2.** idleness; *synonyms* (*n*) ease, torpor, idling, sloth, unemployment, faineance; *antonyms* (*n*) employment, energy.

uhere itch; *synonyms* (*n*) desire, urge, impulse, scabies, wish, longing, craving, fancy, hunger, inclination, itchiness, itching, yearning, yen, (*v*) irritate, tickle, prickle, scratch, tingle, chafe, sting, (*adj*) herpes, heartburn, heaves, hemorrhoids, hernia.

uhiki marriage; *synonyms* (*n*) wedding, matrimony, espousal, nuptial, union, wedlock, alliance, coupling, bond, nuptials, (*adj*) bridal, (*v*) match; *antonyms* (*n*) divorce, separation.

Uiru jealousy; *synonyms* (*n*) suspicion, competition, contention, distrust, qualm, scruple, doubt, challenge, contest, diffidence, dissatisfaction, emulation, enmity, jealoushood, misdoubt, opposition, yellowness, greed, resentment, rivalship, struggle.

Uka come; *synonyms* (*v*) approach, become, aggregate, appear, arise, arrive, fall, befall, amount, descend, get, go, hail, number, originate, reach, rise, spring, total, advance, accrue, be, chance, climax, derive, develop, do, enter, fare, follow; *antonym* (*v*) leave.

UkI honey; *synonyms* (*n*) darling, dear, beloved, love, sweetheart, dearest, duck, baby, molasses, sugar, flame, (*v*) sweeten.

uma 1. go away; *synonyms* (*v*) depart, leave, exit, go, separate, vacate, disappear, vanish, (*int*) away; *antonym* (*v*) stay, **2.** dry up; *synonyms* (*v*) desiccate, shrivel, wither, dehydrate, parch, shrink, wilt, **3.** go out; *synonyms* (*v*) date, ebb, expire, allow, ascertain, assure, attend, bequeath, break, catch, check, consider, construe, control, decease, determine, die, discover, draw, encounter, ensure, entrust, envision, escape, escort, examine, experience, fancy, (*int*) out, begone; *antonym* (*v*) enter.

Umba mould; *synonyms* (*n*) mildew, cast, form, molding, moulding, stamp, modeling, casting, set, fit, punch, (*v*) mold, make, model, frame, fashion, forge, knead, carve, shape, work, hurl, influence.

UmUthi today; *synonyms* (*adv*) now, currently, nowadays, presently, immediately, directly, forthwith, instantly, straightaway, (*n*) present, (*adj*) modern, recent, up-to-date.

una 1. bend; *synonyms* (*n*) bow, arch, arc, elbow, twist, angle, curvature, bending, buckle, flexure, kink, round, (*v*) curve, turn, crouch, stoop, crook, curl, flex, deflect, fold, loop, swerve, wind, contort, cower, deform, distort, hunch, incline; *antonyms* (*v*) straighten, square, **2.** hem; *synonyms* (*n*) edging, border, brim, frame, skirt, verge, seam, list, margin, rim, skirting, trimming, flounce, frill, (*v*) fringe, edge, envelop, hum, tuck.

UndU affair; *synonyms* (*n*) matter, business, concern, event, job, occasion, occurrence, amour, duty, happening, incident, issue, party, subject, theme, thing, topic, transaction, meeting, affaire, case, circumstance, episode, experience, fact, function, liaison, occupation, relationship, (*v*) collision.

ungania collect; *synonyms* (*v*) assemble, accumulate, amass, gather, pick, accrue, acquire, aggregate, cluster, collate, congregate, convene, cull, harvest, hoard, raise, accept, catch, compile, derive, flock, gain, garner, glean, group, levy, marshal, meet, muster, obtain; *antonyms* (*v*) disperse, distribute.

uniu cattle; *synonyms* (*n*) beast, cows, stock, kine, livestock, oxen, sheep, antelopes, bison, camels, crowd, mob, public, barb, bidet, charger, chevrotains, cob, colt, courser, deer, filly, foal, giraffes, goats, goer, hack, horse, horses, hunter.

UnUra 1. shell; *synonyms* (*n*) peel, rind, bullet, case, casing, sheath, bark, carcass, crust, shot, carapace, coat, eggshell, hull, scale, skin, slug, grenade, cortex, coffin, jacket, projectile, exterior, framework, sleeve, (*v*) bomb, bombard, husk, pod, blast, **2.** peel; *synonyms* (*n*) hide, peeling, (*v*) flake, flay, pare, decorticate, excoriate, shave, strip, disrobe, desquamate, scrape, slice, undress.

ura 1. leak; *synonyms* (*n*) leakage, crevice, breach, disclosure, chink, escape, fissure, hole, revelation, crack, flaw, cranny, outflow, puncture, rent, (*v*) dribble, reveal, release, disclose, drip, drop, ooze, trickle, permeate, discharge, divulge, drain, emit, filter, flow, **2.** ooze out; *synonyms* (*v*) exudate, exude, transude.

uraga kill; *synonyms* (*v*) assassinate, destroy, erase, annihilate, eliminate, extinguish, finish, blast, butcher, decimate, dispatch, eradicate, execute, behead, efface, defeat, liquidate, massacre, obliterate, quell, remove, shoot, slaughter, slay, smother, stop, impale, (*n*) murder, game, prey.

urImi agriculture; *synonyms* (*n*) farming, agribusiness, agronomy, husbandry, tillage, geoponics, agriculturism, culture, defense, education, interior, labor, plough, state, terraculture, agronomics, commerce, justice, land, plowland, treasury.

Urio right hand; *synonyms* (*n*) right, clockwise, rightfield, rightfulness.

uriri bed; *synonyms* (*n*) couch, layer, base, basis, berth, bottom, flowerbed, foundation, crib, sack, rest, support, pallet, understructure, setting, course, seam, seat, strata, stratum, underside, (*v*) embed, hump.

UritU 1. rhythm; *synonyms* (*n*) measure, cadence, meter, beat, pulse, cycle, tempo, rhyme, metre, melody, strain, swing, accent, assonance, crambo, flow, foot, inflection, pulsation, **2.** weight; *synonyms* (*n*) load, burden, charge, consequence, heaviness, importance, pressure, significance, stress, ballast, bias, import, influence, moment, emphasis, avoirdupois, force, validity, authority, freight, mass, meaning, weightiness, weighting, power, heft, (*v*) gravity, counterweight, tax, slant; *antonym* (*n*) triviality.

urogi witchcraft; *synonyms* (*n*) magic, incantation, sorcery, witchery, enchantment, spell, fascination, necromancy.

Uru bad; *synonyms* (*adj*) evil, adverse, harmful, immoral, naughty, poisonous, sad, sinister, wicked, malicious, infamous, appalling, awful, damaging, devilish, disagreeable, dreadful, hurtful, ill, mischievous, nasty, negative, off, putrid, rotten, sinful, sorry, stale, (*v*) decayed, rancid; *antonyms* (*adj*) fresh, pleasant, well, well-behaved, (*n*) good; **nunga Uru** smell.

uruga stir; *synonyms* (*v*) arouse, budge, move, rouse, affect, agitate, excite, inspire, go, cause, foment,

shift, actuate, animate, awaken, beat, disturb, (*n*) movement, commotion, disturbance, excitement, agitation, fuss, riot, tumult, ferment, ado, din, disorder, (*adj*) bustle.

uruhi palm; *synonyms* (*n*) decoration, medal, prize, thenar, victory, medallion, (*v*) hand, filch, bag, cabbage, crib, handle, nim, pilfer, rob.

Uta 1. bowstring; *synonyms* (*n*) noose, drop, gallows, halter, rope, tree, (*v*) behead, gibbet, electrocute, hang, strangle, **2.** bending; *synonyms* (*n*) bend, bow, flexion, deflection, deflexion, crook, flexure, (*adj*) flexible, supple, pliant, winding, **3.** bow; *synonyms* (*n*) arc, curve, obeisance, turn, curvature, stem, vault, head, nose, beak, hook, bowing, bowknot, fore, front, (*v*) arch, stoop, duck, buckle, crouch, incline, kowtow, defer, kneel, nod, submit, bob, squat, sag, couch.

uthayo 1. idleness; *synonyms* (*n*) ease, laziness, lethargy, torpor, idling, inaction, inactivity, inertia, sloth, unemployment, faineance; *antonyms* (*n*) employment, energy, **2.** sloth; *synonyms* (*n*) idleness, indolence, acedia, listlessness, slothfulness.

utheri 1. sky; *synonyms* (*n*) air, heaven, atmosphere, heavens, space, distance, (*v*) fling, flip, pitch, agitate, alternate, cant, chuck, convulse, deliver, discard, dispose, flick, gear, hawk, huckster, incline, interchange, jerk, jump, leaf, lurch, monger, peddle, riffle, **2.** light; *synonyms* (*adj*) fair, clear, facile, easy, faint, flimsy, airy, bright, clean, dizzy, fine, frivolous, gentle, (*n*) flame, brightness, daylight, illumination, dawn, (*v*) fire, kindle, inflame, glow, ignite, dismount, illuminate, enkindle, alight, brighten, descend, fall; *antonyms* (*adj*) fattening, nauseating, (*n*) dark, darkness, gloom, shade, night, (*v*) extinguish, darken, (*alt sp*) heavy; **utheri wa mweri** moonlight.

uthiu face; *synonyms* (*n*) look, aspect, countenance, expression, side, top, exterior, appearance, facade, surface, boldness, brass, cheek, effrontery, facing, grimace, impudence, (*v*) confront, audacity, veneer, visage, affront, breast, defy, brave, cover, encounter, endure, meet, (*adj*) front; *antonyms* (*v*) avoid, back.

uthondeki medicine; *synonyms* (*n*) cure, drug, medicament, medication, physic, remedy, therapy, treatment, cathartic, potion, preparation, antidote, (*v*) medicate.

UtukU night; *synonyms* (*n*) dark, evening, dusk, darkness, nighttime, twilight, (*adj*) nocturnal; *antonyms* (*n*) day, light.

wonje cripple; *synonyms* (*n*) invalid, (*v*) lame, maim, mutilate, damage, enfeeble, incapacitate, injure, weaken, becripple, (*adj*) paralyze, prostrate.

V

vUciU tomorrow; *synonyms* (*adv*) kal, never.

W

wambui micore zebra; *synonym* (*n*) referee.
we he; *synonyms* (*pron*) cestui, (*n*) male, man, helium.
wega good; *synonyms* (*adj*) able, benefit, delicious, right, efficient, capable, excellent, fine, nice, superior, well, advantageous, agreeable, desirable, generous, gentle, admirable, beneficent, beneficial, benevolent, estimable, fair, friendly, full, pleasing, respectable, upright, (*n*) benign, advantage, gain; *antonyms* (*adj*) disobedient, poor, wicked, unpleasant, (*n*) evil, bad.
wendo 1. zeal; *synonyms* (*n*) ardor, eagerness, fervor, devotion, enthusiasm, passion, vehemence, fire, fervency, heat, fervour, ardour, elan, keenness, earnestness, fanaticism, gusto, animation, fervidness, zest, avidity, excitement, impetuosity, industry, love, promptness, (*v*) empressement, gush; *antonyms* (*n*) indifference, apathy, **2.** want; *synonyms* (*v*) need, desire, require, like, hope, crave, covet, (*n*) lack, poverty, wish, deficiency, deprivation, famine, absence, dearth, demand, destitution, indigence, necessity, penury, privation, shortage, pauperism, defect, requirement, distress, ambition, fancy, essential, hardship; *antonyms* (*v*) dislike, hate, **3.** love; *synonyms* (*n*) affection, dear, fondness, liking, benevolence, charity, attachment, beloved, darling, honey, sweetheart, favor, beau, adoration, friendship, pet, regard, tenderness, amour, heart, partiality, grace, (*v*) cherish, enjoy, worship, adore, affect, treasure, choose, (*adj*) flame; *antonyms* (*n*) abhorrence, hatred, aversion, (*v*) abhor, **4.** eagerness; *synonyms* (*n*) aspiration, cupidity, avidness, readiness, zeal, greediness, hunger, impatience, longing, thirst, warmth, (*v*) craving.
wIra work; *synonyms* (*n*) exercise, business, employment, function, task, action, act, book, composition, occupation, service, writing, office, deed, (*v*) labor, operate, toil, cultivate, exploit, ferment, form, manipulate, operation, run, serve, use, produce, do, (*adj*) job, trade; *antonyms* (*v*) idle, malfunction.
wIru ripe; *synonyms* (*adj*) mature, adult, ready, advanced, good, prepared, perfect, matured, consummate, right, (*v*) mellow; *antonym* (*adj*) green.

Index of English Subjects to Kikuyu Subjects

A

abound *see* kUiyUra.
above *see* igUrU.
abscess *see* mahUha.
abstain *see* kwihutia.
abundant *see* nyingI.
abuse *see* ruma.
accommodation *see* kIraro.
act *see* gIko.
add up *see* 1. Iara, 2. taranIria.
affair *see* 1. maIndU, 2. UndU.
agriculture *see* urImi.
all *see* ciothe.
alter *see* gUcenjia.
animal *see* nyamu.
answer *see* cokia ciuria.
ape *see* nugU.
appoint *see* 1. cagUra, 2. thura.
arm *see* 1. guoko, 2. rUhI.
armpit *see* njegeke.
arrange *see* 1. banga, 2. thondeka, 3. thondekania.
arrest *see* kunyita.
arrive *see* 1. gukinya, 2. kinya.
arrow *see* mUgwI.
ascend *see* 1. ambata, 2. haita.
ashes *see* mUku.
ask for *see* hoya.
assemble *see* kungania.
aunt *see* tata.
avoid *see* girIrIria.
axe *see* ithanwa.

B

baboon *see* nugU.
back *see* thutha; go back coka.
backbone *see* mukummuthu.
bad *see* 1. Uru, 2. njUru, 3. kIUru, 4. mUUru.
bale *see* kIohe.
banana *see* 1. irigU, 2. muramba.
bark *see* ikoni.

barren *see* 1. kUhinja, 2. thata.
bask *see* ota.
bathe *see* kwiyoga.
be born *see* ciarwo.
be quiet *see* kira.
beach *see* hUgUrUru.
bead *see* 1. ciUma, 2. mUgathi.
beard *see* nderu.
beat *see* hura.
beautiful *see* thaka.
bed *see* uriri.
bedstead *see* kangamia.
bee *see* njUkI.
beer *see* njohi.
befit *see* agIrIra.
belly *see* nda.
below *see* 1. ndaruI, 2. rungu.
bend *see* 1. gurya, 2. una, 3. inamIrIria, 4. kUnja.
bending *see* Uta.
bewitch *see* roga.
bifurcation *see* macamanio.
bile *see* nyongo.
bird *see* nyoni; bird of prey nderi.
bite *see* rUma.
bitter *see* ngagatu.
black *see* nduma njirU.
bladder *see* thUngi.
blind *see* thukia; blind person mUtumumu.
blind person *see* mUtumumu.
blood *see* thakame.
blow up *see* huuha.
boast *see* gwItIa kwIgana.
boat *see* itarU.
body *see* mwIrI.
boil *see* 1. cemUra, 2. hiUhia, 3. mahUha.
bond servant *see* ngombo.
bone *see* ihindi.
border *see* kuhakana.
borrow *see* 1. gUkomba, 2. he, 3. kombera.
bottle *see* cuba.
boundary *see* muhaka.
bow *see* Uta.
bowstring *see* Uta.
brag *see* gwItIa kwIgana.
brain *see* tombo.
branch *see* rUhonge.
brass *see* gicango; brass wire gicango.
brass wire *see* gicango.
bread *see* mUgate.
break *see* kuuraga; break wind girIrIria rUhuho.
break wind *see* girIrIria rUhuho.
breast *see* iria.
breath *see* huma.
breathe *see* hUmUka.

breathing *see* huma.
bridge *see* **1**. itiki, **2**. mUgogo.
bring *see* rehe; **bring up** gukuria.
bring up *see* gukuria.
broom *see* kInato.
broth *see* thathi.
brother *see* **1**. mUndU witU, **2**. mUrUwa maitU.
bruise *see* kuhoruhia.
buffalo *see* mbogo.
build *see* aka.
bull *see* ndegwa.
bunch *see* ikundo.
bundle *see* kIohe.
burden *see* murigo.
burn *see* cina.
bury *see* thika.
bush *see* gIthaka.
butterfly *see* kihuruta.
buttermilk *see* thagi.
buttocks *see* itina.
buy *see* kUgUra.

C

calabash *see* kinya.
calf *see* njau.
call *see* Ita.
canine tooth *see* gathanda mboiro.
canoe *see* itarU; **dugout canoe** gatarU.
care for *see* **1**. menyerera, **2**. rIithia.
carry *see* **1**. kuua, **2**. oya.
cat *see* nyau.
cattle *see* uniu.
cease *see* gUthira.
centipede *see* mUnyongoro.
change *see* **1**. cenjia, **2**. garUra, **3**. gUcenjia.
charcoal *see* ikara.
chase *see* hanyUkia.
cheek *see* kireru.
chest *see* **1**. gIthUri, **2**. gIthUru.
chief *see* mUnene.
child *see* mwana.
chin *see* kireru.
choose *see* thuura.
clan *see* mbari.
climb *see* **1**. ambata, **2**. haita.
close *see* **1**. gUtumia kanua, **2**. kUhinga maitho, **3**. kuhingira.
cloth *see* ngora.
clothe *see* **1**. humba, **2**. Ikira.
clothes *see* ngu.
cloud *see* matu.

coagulate *see* kUganda.
coast *see* hUgUrUru.
cohabit *see* inglrIna.
cold *see* heho.
collect *see* **1**. kungania, **2**. ungania.
come *see* Uka; **come in** ingIra.
come in *see* ingIra.
complete *see* rikia.
compose *see* gutukania.
construct *see* **1**. aka, **2**. thondeka.
cook *see* ruga.
cool *see* kuhonia.
copper *see* gicango.
cork *see* **1**. gIkunIko, **2**. ngunIko.
corpse *see* **1**. kIimba, **2**. nnukuU.
cough *see* korora.
country *see* bUrUrI.
courtyard *see* nja.
cover *see* humbIra.
cow *see* ng'ombe.
coward *see* kIguoya.
crack *see* atUra.
crawl *see* kuruma.
creep *see* kuruma.
cripple *see* wonje.
crocodile *see* kIngangi.
cross *see* ringa.
crossroads *see* macamanio.
crow *see* igogo.
cry *see* **1**. mUrIro, **2**. rIra.
cultivate *see* kurIma.
curdled milk *see* iria imata.
cure *see* kuhonia.
cut *see* tinia.

D

dance *see* **1**. kUina, **2**. kwIgangara.
dark *see* nduma njirU.
darkness *see* nduma.
date palm *see* ndende.
day *see* mUthenya.
daytime *see* muthenya.
dead person *see* **1**. fUmba, **2**. kIimba.
death *see* gIkuU; **put to death** kUraga.
decisive *see* kUrIkia.
decorate *see* gemia.
deny *see* kara.
destroy *see* thUkia.
detest *see* mena.
dew *see* ime.
die *see* kua.

dig *see* cimba; **dig up** cimbUria; **dig out** cimbUria.
dig out *see* cimbUria.
dig up *see* cimbUria.
diminish *see* nyiha.
dirt *see* gIko.
disappear *see* kurira.
disembodied spirit *see* huho.
disgrace *see* thoni.
display *see* onania.
distress *see* 1. thIna, 2. manyamaro.
district *see* bUrUrI.
divide *see* gayania.
divorce *see* gUtigana.
do *see* 1. Ika, 2. rikia, 3. ruta.
dog *see* 1. ngitI, 2. ngui.
donkey *see* ndigiri.
door *see* murango.
drag *see* 1. gucia, 2. kururia.
draw *see* gutaha maI.
dream *see* 1. kiroto, 2. rota.
drink *see* nyua.
drizzle *see* rUthuthuU.
drop *see* gUithia.
drum *see* kihembe.
dry *see* nyUmU; **dry up** Uma; **dry land** nyUmU.
dry land *see* nyUmU.
dry up *see* Uma.
duck *see* mbata.
dugout canoe *see* gatarU.
dull *see* 1. nditU, 2. ritU.
dung *see* mai.
dust *see* 1. rubiri, 2. rUkUngU.
dwell *see* kUUra.

E

eagerness *see* wendo.
eagle *see* nderi.
ear *see* gUtU.
egg *see* itumbI.
eight *see* inyanya.
elbow *see* kIgokora.
elephant *see* njogu.
enclosure *see* rUgiri.
escape *see* 1. honoka, 2. hona.
evil spirit *see* ngoma.
examine *see* 1. thima, 2. rora.
excellent *see* ega makIria.
excrement *see* mai.
exercise *see* ruta ngoma.
explain *see* tarIria.
extinguish *see* nyotoka.

eye *see* ritho.
eyebrow *see* rUbutu.
eyelash *see* 1. ngobe, 2. rUkobe.

F

face *see* uthiu.
fade *see* kurira.
faint *see* 1. kuregera, 2. kUringIka.
fall *see* gua.
fan *see* hurutIra.
far *see* haraya.
fat *see* 1. kUnora, 2. noru.
father *see* baba.
fear *see* guoya.
fence *see* rUgiri.
ferment *see* 1. gagata, 2. kUganda.
fetch *see* rehe.
fierce *see* njugI.
fight *see* hurara.
fill *see* iyuria.
filter *see* cunga.
filth *see* gIko.
final *see* kUrIkia.
fine *see* ega makIria.
finger *see* rIara.
fingernail *see* rwara.
finish *see* 1. gUthira, 2. rikia.
fire *see* mwaki; **set on fire** akia mundia.
fireplace *see* riko.
firewood *see* ngU.
fish *see* 1. tega, 2. kIUngUyU.
fishing line *see* ndUaro.
fist *see* ngundi.
five *see* ithano.
flock *see* gIkundi.
flutter *see* batabata.
fly *see* kumbuka; **tsetse fly** mbogo kenyarare.
foam *see* muhUyU.
follow *see* 1. rUmanIrIra, 2. rUmIrIra.
foot *see* 1. ikinya, 2. kUgUrU.
forest *see* mUtitU.
forge *see* kUnja.
four *see* inya.
fowl *see* ngUkU; **guinea fowl** Nganga.
frog *see* kIura.
fruit *see* itunda.
fry *see* karanga.
fur *see* njoya.
furrow *see* mutaro.

G

garbage *see* 1. gIko, 2. mahuti.
garden *see* mUgUnda.
gas *see* mIrukI.
gather *see* getha.
get well *see* 1. hora, 2. hona.
ghost *see* kloneki.
giraffe *see* muitirira.
girl *see* mUirItu.
give *see* nengera; **give away** heana.
give away *see* heana.
glare *see* rora.
glide *see* nyUrUrUka.
go *see* thiI; **go out** thiI; **go in** ingIra; **go back** coka;
    go away thiI.
go away *see* 1. uma, 2. thiI.
go back *see* coka.
go in *see* ingIra.
go out *see* 1. thiI, 2. uma.
goat *see* mbUri.
good *see* wega.
grace *see* 1. kUrUta, 2. huura.
grain *see* hindi.
grandfather *see* guka.
grandmother *see* cUcU.
grasp *see* 1. mbata, 2. kumbata.
grass *see* nyeki; **blade of grass** ithangu.
grate *see* kUrUta.
great *see* 1. nene, 2. munene.
grief *see* kIeha.
grind *see* kia.
groan *see* rUara.
groove *see* mutaro.
group *see* gIkundi.
grow *see* kumera; **grow up** gUkUra.
grow up *see* gUkUra.
gruel *see* ucUrU.
grumble *see* nuguna.
grunt *see* nuguna.
guest *see* mUgeni.
guinea fowl *see* Nganga.
gun *see* mUcinga.

handle *see* 1. mUtI, 2. nyitIro.
hard *see* nyUmU.
hardship *see* 1. manyamaro, 2. thIna.
hare *see* mbuku.
harmonise *see* gutwarana.
haste *see* narua.
hate *see* mena.
hay *see* mahuti.
he *see* we.
head *see* 1. mUtwe, 2. kIongo.
heal *see* kuhonia.
heap *see* 1. hUmba, 2. kihUmba; **rubbish heap**
    kIara; **heap up** akia mundia.
heap up *see* 1. akia mundia, 2. cina.
hear *see* Igua.
heart *see* ngoro.
hearth *see* riko.
heavy *see* 1. nditU, 2. ritU.
heel *see* muthimimo.
heifer *see* ndegwa.
held *see* kunyita.
hem *see* una.
hen *see* ngUkU.
here *see* haha.
hiccup *see* kiengetha.
hide *see* hitha.
highest point *see* 1. gacUmbiri, 2. mUthia.
highway *see* njIra.
hill *see* karima.
hip *see* ita.
hippopotamus *see* nguU.
hoe *see* icembe.
hole *see* 1. gItara, 2. irima.
home *see* mucii.
honey *see* UkI.
honor *see* tia.
hook *see* inamIrIria.
horn *see* muguongo.
horse *see* mbarathi.
house *see* nyumba.
hump *see* 1. iguku, 2. igungu.
hundred *see* igana.
hunger *see* 1. hUta, 2. ng'araga.
hunt *see* 1. guIma, 2. hIta.
hunting *see* 1. ihIta, 2. iguImia.
husband *see* mUrUme.
hut *see* muthonge.
hyena *see* hiti.

H

haft *see* 1. mUtI, 2. nyitIro.
hair *see* njuIrI.
hand *see* 1. rUhI, 2. guoko; **right hand** Urio.

I

idleness *see* 1. UgUta, 2. uthayo.
imagine *see* gwIciria.
imitate *see* mwIgere kanio.
increase *see* ongerera.
inheritance *see* igai.
inside *see* 1. gatagatI, 2. thIinI, 3. thIni.
instruct *see* rutana.
iron *see* kigera; **iron ore** kIgera.
iron ore *see* kIgera.
itch *see* uhere.
ivory *see* muguongo.

J

jaw *see* ngambucu.
jealousy *see* Uiru.
jerk *see* 1. makia, 2. thitUra.
journey *see* rUgendo.
judge *see* mUtuithania.
jump *see* rIga.

K

kidney *see* itigo.
kill *see* uraga.
king *see* muthamaki.
kitchen *see* riko.
kite *see* 1. hUngU, 2. rUIgI.
knead *see* kanda.
knee *see* iru.
kneel *see* turia ndu.
knife *see* kahiU.
knit *see* tuma.
knock *see* ringa.
knot *see* ikundo.
know *see* menya.

L

lake *see* iria.
lamp *see* tawa.
land *see* 1. gIthaka, 2. mUgUnda; **dry land** nyUmU.

large *see* nene.
laugh *see* theka.
lazy *see* gUthaya.
leaf *see* ithangu.
leak *see* 1. ita, 2. ura.
lean *see* kuunamirira; **lean on** komera.
lean on *see* komera.
leap *see* rIga.
learn *see* kwirUta.
leave *see* 1. thiI, 2. tiga, 3. rUtha.
leg *see* 1. kUgUrU, 2. ikinya.
lend *see* 1. he, 2. kombera.
leopard *see* ngarI.
lick *see* gucuna.
lie down *see* koma.
lift up *see* oyana igUrU.
light *see* utheri.
lightning *see* ruheni.
line *see* muhari; **fishing line** ndUaro.
lion *see* mUrUthi.
lip *see* kIromo.
listen *see* thikIrIria.
liver *see* ini.
load *see* murigo.
locust *see* ngigi.
long *see* ndaya.
look after *see* 1. menyerera, 2. rIithia.
look at *see* rora.
look for *see* gucaria.
louse *see* ndaa.
love *see* 1. kwenda, 2. wendo.
lung *see* ihUri.

M

machine *see* kIgera.
magic *see* 1. kIama, 2. Ugo.
maize *see* bembe.
male *see* njamba.
many *see* nyIngi.
marriage *see* uhiki.
marry *see* hikania.
master *see* 1. mUnene, 2. mwathi.
match *see* gutwarana.
material *see* ngu.
mature *see* thumu.
measure *see* 1. gIthimi, 2. thima.
meat *see* nyama.
medicine *see* 1. muthaiga, 2. uthondeki; **medicine man** ihUragUri.
medicine man *see* ihUragUri.
meet *see* tUnga.

melt *see* gUtwekia.
metal pot *see* mukebe.
midwife *see* mUciarithania.
migrate *see* thama.
milk *see* **1**. hiha, **2**. iria, **3**. kama; **curdled milk** iria imata.
millipede *see* munyongoro.
mire *see* ndoro.
mix *see* **1**. tukania, **2**. thombocania.
modesty *see* thoni.
monk *see* **1**. ngIma, **2**. nUgU, **3**. theerI.
moon *see* mweri.
mosquito *see* rUmuru.
mother *see* maitu.
mould *see* Umba.
mountain *see* kIrIma.
mourning *see* girIka.
mouth *see* kanua.
movement *see* mUthiIne.
mud *see* ndoro.
mug *see* **1**. gIkombe, **2**. mUkebe.
mushroom *see* makunU.

N

name *see* ritwa.
navel *see* mukonyo.
near *see* hakuhI.
neck *see* ngingo.
need *see* **1**. bata, **2**. kwenda.
nest *see* **1**. gItara, **2**. irima.
new *see* njerU.
night *see* UtukU.
nine *see* kenda.
nose *see* inUrU.

O

oar *see* mwIiko.
offspring *see* njiarwo.
oil *see* maguta.
old *see* **1**. kUra, **2**. ngUru; **old times** tene; **old person** mUndU mUkUrU.
old person *see* mUndU mUkUrU.
old times *see* tene.
one *see* Imwe.
ooze out *see* **1**. ita, **2**. ura.
open *see* kuhingura; **open space** kieni.
open space *see* kieni.
ostrich *see* nyaga.

outside *see* nja.
overcome *see* **1**. cinda, **2**. kuhota.

P

pack *see* **1**. cokanIriria, **2**. gIkundi, **3**. kIohe, **4**. kuoha mIrigo.
paddle *see* itanga.
palm *see* uruhi; **date palm** ndende.
parrot *see* gathuku.
pass *see* hItUka.
path *see* gacIra.
pay *see* rIha.
peak *see* muthia.
peel *see* UnUra.
peg *see* ruambo.
penetrate *see* ingIra thIini.
penis *see* mUthita.
permission *see* rUtha.
person *see* mUndU; **old person** mUndU mUkUrU; **dead person** fUmba; **blind person** mUtumumu.
pestle *see* mUUthI.
pick up *see* oyana igUrU.
pile up *see* **1**. hUmba, **2**. iganIrIra.
pinch *see* cecenia.
pit *see* irima.
place *see* **1**. iga, **2**. ikira, **3**. handu.
plait *see* kundika.
plant *see* handa.
pleasant *see* mUrio.
please *see* keria.
point *see* muthia; **highest point** gacUmbiri.
pool *see* ndia.
porcupine *see* njege.
porridge *see* ngima.
pot *see* **1**. nyUngU, **2**. thaburia, **3**. gIkombe, **4**. mUkebe; **metal pot** mukebe.
pound *see* konyora.
pour *see* ita.
power *see* hinga.
powerful *see* munene.
pregnancy *see* **1**. nda, **2**. ihu.
prepare *see* thondeka.
press out *see* hiha.
produce *see* onania.
pronounce *see* **1**. gweta, **2**. tamUka.
province *see* bUrUrI.
pull *see* **1**. gucia, **2**. kururia; **pull up** gucia; **pull out** gucia.
pull out *see* gucia.
pull up *see* **1**. gucia, **2**. rugama.
pump *see* mbombo.

push *see* gUtindika.
put *see* 1. iga, 2. ikira; **put together** aka; **put to death** kUraga; **put right** thondeka; **put out** rutanja.
put out *see* rutanja.
put right *see* thondeka.
put together *see* 1. aka, 2. tukania, 3. gutukania, 4. thondeka.
python *see* itarara.

Q

quarrel *see* negenania.
quench *see* nyotoka.

R

rain *see* mbura.
rainy season *see* muringo.
razor *see* kanyui.
read *see* thoma.
reap *see* getha.
receive *see* amUkIra.
recover *see* 1. hona, 2. honoka.
refuse *see* 1. rega, 2. regana.
reject *see* regana.
relative *see* 1. mUndU witU, 2. mUrUwa maitU.
remain *see* 1. gUtigwo, 2. ikara.
remedy *see* muthaiga.
remember *see* ririkana.
remove *see* tegura.
repair *see* thondeka.
request *see* bata.
resemble *see* 1. hanana, 2. hinanana, 3. kUhanana.
rest *see* 1. hurUka, 2. kuruka, 3. hUmUka.
return *see* coka.
reveal *see* kuguuria.
rhinoceros *see* huria.
rhythm *see* UritU.
rib *see* rUbaru.
right hand *see* Urio.
ripe *see* wIru.
ripen *see* kwIrua.
roar *see* kurarama.
roast *see* 1. cina, 2. hihia, 3. hIhihia.
rooster *see* njambe.
root *see* mUri.
rotten *see* 1. thUka, 2. ora, 3. thUko, 4. kuora, 5. njoru.
row *see* muhari.

rub *see* kuhura.
rubbish *see* 1. gIko, 2. mahuti; **rubbish heap** kIara.
rubbish heap *see* kIara.
rumble *see* kurarama.
run *see* teng'era.

S

sacrifice *see* igongona.
salt *see* mUnyU.
sand *see* tIIri.
satisfy *see* 1. hunia, 2. igania, 3. keria.
scatter *see* kUharagara.
scorpion *see* kangaUrU.
scrape *see* 1. huura, 2. kUrUta.
scratch *see* kUrUta.
scythe *see* rUhiU.
see *see* ona.
seed *see* mbegU.
seize *see* kUnyita.
self *see* mwene.
sell *see* kwendia.
send *see* tUma; **send away** eheria.
send away *see* 1. eheria, 2. heana rutha.
separate *see* gUtigana.
serious *see* 1. nditU, 2. ritU.
serpent *see* nyamU yathI.
set *see* 1. iga, 2. kUratha; **set up** cagUra; **set on fire** akia mundia.
set up *see* 1. cagUra, 2. thura.
seven *see* mugwanja.
sew *see* tuma.
shade *see* kIruru.
shadow *see* kIruru.
shake *see* kUinaina.
shame *see* 1. conoka, 2. thoni.
sharp *see* njugI.
sharpen *see* kunora.
shave *see* kwenya.
sheep *see* ng'ondu.
shell *see* UnUra.
shield *see* ngo.
shin *see* giciri.
shiver *see* 1. anaina, 2. inaina.
short *see* nguhI.
shoulder *see* kiande.
shout *see* anirIra.
shudder *see* inaina.
sick *see* rwara.
sickle *see* rUhiU.
sift *see* gucunga.
sing *see* ina.

singe *see* cina.
sink *see* 1. tonyerera, 2. gutuamo.
sit *see* ikarathI.
six *see* iihathatu.
size *see* gIthimi.
skin *see* 1. gIkonde, 2. ikoro.
sky *see* 1. igUrU, 2. utheri.
slander *see* cambia.
slap *see* gUtha rUhi.
slash *see* 1. gUtinia, 2. tinia.
slaughter *see* thinja.
slave *see* ngombo.
sleep *see* 1. koma toro, 2. toro.
slip *see* gutenderUka.
slope *see* kuunamirira.
sloth *see* 1. UgUta, 2. uthayo.
slug *see* ndimbo.
small *see* nini.
smallpox *see* 1. muhane, 2. mUthandUkU.
smell *see* 1. nunga Uru, 2. nunga wesa; **smell out** kunungira.
smell out *see* kunungira.
smoke *see* ndogo.
snail *see* 1. ndimbo, 2. ndinoho.
snake *see* nyamU yathI.
snap *see* kuuraga.
snare *see* mutego.
sneeze *see* gwathimUra.
sniff *see* kunungira.
snore *see* ng'orota.
snort *see* ng'orota.
soil *see* tIIri.
song *see* rwImbo.
soot *see* mUrari.
sorcerer *see* murogi.
sore *see* kionda.
sorrow *see* kIeha.
soul *see* 1. ngoro, 2. roho.
sound *see* mUrIro.
sow *see* handa.
spark *see* thandI.
speak *see* arla.
spear *see* itimu.
sperm *see* mbegu.
spirit *see* 1. ngoma, 2. ngoro, 3. roho; **evil spirit** ngoma; **disembodied spirit** huho.
spit *see* tua mata.
spitting cobra *see* gIIko.
spittle *see* mata.
splice *see* gwatania.
split *see* atUra.
spoil *see* thUkia.
spoon *see* gIciko.
spread *see* 1. anika, 2. haka, 3. kUharagara.

spring *see* 1. gutUma, 2. kIgera.
squeeze *see* 1. hiha, 2. kama; **squeeze out** kuhiha.
squeeze out *see* kuhiha.
squirrel *see* gaturu.
stack *see* 1. hUmba, 2. iganIrIra.
star *see* njata.
stare *see* rora.
startle *see* 1. makia, 2. thitUra.
stay *see* tigwo.
steal *see* iya.
steel *see* cuma.
stick *see* mUkuanju.
stir *see* 1. kuuruga, 2. uruga; **stir up** kuuruga.
stir up *see* 1. kuuruga, 2. kuurugira.
stomach *see* nda.
stone *see* ihiga.
stop up *see* guthika.
stopper *see* 1. gIkunIko, 2. ngunIko.
strain *see* cunga.
stranger *see* mUgeni.
strength *see* hinga.
strike *see* ringa.
string *see* rurigi.
stumble *see* hingwo.
suck *see* onga.
suffer *see* gukiririra.
sugar cane *see* kIgwa.
suit *see* agIrIra.
surpass *see* hItUka.
surround *see* gUthiUrUrUka.
swallow *see* meria.
swear *see* hita.
sweat *see* thigino.
sweep *see* hata; **sweep up** hata.
sweep up *see* hata.
sweet *see* mUrio; **sweet potato** ngwaci.
sweet potato *see* ngwaci.
swell *see* imba.
sword *see* njora.

T

tail *see* 1. mUcuthi, 2. mutingoe.
take *see* 1. kuua, 2. oya; **take off** ruta; **take in** kwanIrIria; **take care** menyerera.
take care *see* menyerera.
take in *see* kwanIrIria.
take off *see* ruta.
taste *see* 1. mUcamo, 2. gUcama.
teach *see* rutana.
tears *see* maithori.
ten *see* ikumi.

test *see* thima.
testicle *see* nyee.
thatched roof *see* mambarita.
there *see* haria.
thick *see* kUnora.
thicket *see* gIthaka.
thief *see* muici.
thigh *see* kIero.
thing *see* kIndU.
think *see* gwIciria.
thirst *see* nyota.
thorn *see* muigwa.
threaten *see* makia.
three *see* ithatu.
tip *see* muthia.
to add up *see* 1. Iara, 2. taranIria.
to ask for *see* hoya.
to assemble *see* kungania.
to break wind *see* girIrIria rUhuho.
to bring *see* rehe; **bring up** gukuria.
to bring up *see* gukuria.
to cohabit *see* ingIrIna.
to come *see* Uka; **come in** ingIra.
to come in *see* ingIra.
to decorate *see* gemia.
to deny *see* kara.
to dig out *see* cimbUria.
to dig up *see* cimbUria.
to get well *see* 1. hora, 2. hona.
to give away *see* heana.
to go back *see* coka.
to go in *see* ingIra.
to grow up *see* gUkUra.
to harmonise *see* gutwarana.
to heap up *see* 1. akia mundia, 2. cina.
to lean on *see* komera.
to lift up *see* oyana igUrU.
to listen *see* thikIrIria.
to migrate *see* thama.
to ooze out *see* 1. ita, 2. ura.
to penetrate *see* ingIra thIini.
to pile up *see* 1. hUmba, 2. iganIrIria.
to press out *see* hiha.
to pull out *see* gucia.
to pull up *see* 1. gucia, 2. rugama.
to recover *see* 1. hona, 2. honoka.
to remember *see* ririkana.
to send *see* tUma; **send away** eheria.
to send away *see* 1. eheria, 2. heana rutha.
to smell out *see* kunungira.
to squeeze out *see* kuhiha.
to stop up *see* guthika.
to sweep up *see* hata.
to take off *see* ruta.

to turn over *see* inamia.
to uncover *see* kuguuria.
to urinate *see* thuguma.
to wrap up *see* oha.
tobacco *see* mbakI; **tobacco pipe** gIIko.
tobacco pipe *see* gIIko.
today *see* UmUthi.
toe *see* kiara.
tomato *see* nyanya.
tomorrow *see* vUciU.
tongue *see* rUrImI.
tooth *see* igego; **canine tooth** gathanda mboiro.
top *see* muthia.
tortoise *see* nguru.
town *see* itura.
trap *see* mutego.
travel *see* guthIIna.
tree *see* mUti.
tremble *see* kUinaina.
trickle *see* nyUrUrUka.
trunk *see* mUguongo.
try *see* geria.
tsetse fly *see* mbogo kenyarare.
turn over *see* inamia.
twin *see* mahatha.
twist *see* 1. gonyaria, 2. inamIrIria, 3. kUnja, 4. nyogonda.
two *see* igIrI.

U

udder *see* mUkamo.
uncooked *see* njIthi.
uncover *see* kuguuria.
underneath *see* 1. rungu, 2. nduruI.
unripe *see* njIthi.
up *see* igUrU; **blow up** huuha; **bring up** gukuria; **dig up** cimbUria; **dry up** Uma; **grow up** gUkUra; **heap up** akia mundia; **lift up** oyana igUrU; **add up** Iara; **pile up** hUmba; **wrap up** oha.
upright *see* naigUrU.
urinate *see* thuguma.
urine *see* mathuguno.
use *see* hUthIra.
utmost *see* 1. gacUmbiri, 2. mUthia.

V

vanquish *see* **1.** kuhota, **2.** cinda.
vapour *see* mIrukI.
vein *see* mUkiha.
vessel *see* **1.** nyUngU, **2.** thaburia.
village *see* gicagi.
virgin *see* mUirItu.
vision *see* kioneki.
voice *see* mUgambo.
vomit *see* tahika.

W

wail *see* rIra.
walk *see* cera.
wall *see* rUthingo.
want *see* **1.** kwenda, **2.** wendo.
war *see* mbara.
wart hog *see* ngIri.
wash *see* **1.** hUra, **2.** thambia.
water *see* maI.
wave *see* **1.** hurutIra, **2.** tegura.
weak *see* **1.** kuregera, **2.** moca.
wear *see* IkIra.
weave *see* tuma.
weight *see* UritU.
well *see* gIthima; **get well** hona.
whistling *see* **1.** hUna, **2.** kIhUni.
white *see* njeru; **white man** mundu mweru.
white man *see* mundu mweru.
who *see* nU.
wicked *see* **1.** agana, **2.** kwagana.
win *see* **1.** cinda, **2.** kuhota.
wind *see* huhuho; **wind up** kuogotha; **break wind**
    girIrIria rUhuho.
wind up *see* **1.** kuogotha, **2.** kwogothithama.
winnow *see* kuheheta.
wipe *see* huura.
wish *see* kwenda.
witchcraft *see* urogi.
woman *see* mUtuma.
womb *see* ihu.
word *see* kiugo.
work *see* wIra.
wrap up *see* oha.
wring *see* kamUra.
wrinkled *see* kuhuhunyana.

Y

yawn *see* mIeU.
year *see* mwaka.
yesterday *see* ira.
young man *see* mwanake.
youth *see* mUndU mwithI.

Z

zeal *see* wendo.
zebra *see* wambui micore.

Vocabulary Study Lists

Verbs (Kikuyu - English)

Kikuyu	English
akia mundia	heap up
amUkIra	receive
cimbUria	dig up
cina	heap up
cinda	vanquish
coka	go back
eheria	send away
gemia	decorate
girIrIria	avoid
girIrIria rUhuho	break wind
gucaria	look for
gUcenjia	alter
gucia	pull up
gukinya	arrive
gukiririra	suffer
gUkUra	grow up
gukuria	bring up
guthika	stop up
gutwarana	harmonise
gwIciria	think
hata	sweep up
he	lend
heana	give away
heana rutha	send away
hiha	press out
hItUka	surpass
hona	recover
honoka	recover
hora	get well
hoya	ask for
hUmba	pile up
Iara	add up
iganIrIra	pile up
Igua	hear
ikarathI	sit
inamia	turn over
ingIra	come in
ingIra thIini	penetrate
ingIrIna	cohabit
ita	ooze out
kanda	knead
kara	deny
kinya	arrive
kombera	lend
komera	lean on
kuguuria	reveal
kuhiha	squeeze out
kuhota	vanquish
kumera	grow
kungania	assemble
kunungira	smell out
kUnyita	seize
kuogotha	wind up
kurira	disappear
kuua	carry
kuuruga	stir up
kuurugira	stir up
kwanIrIria	take in
kwirUta	learn
kwogothithama	wind up
makia	threaten
menyerera	take care
nyotoka	extinguish
oha	wrap up
oya	carry
oyana igUrU	lift up
regana	reject
rehe	bring
ririkana	remember
rora	look at
rugama	pull up
ruta	take off
rutana	instruct
taranIria	add up
tarIria	explain
thama	migrate
thiI	go out
thikIrIria	listen
thima	examine

thoma	read	heap up	akia mundia
thondeka	put right	hear	Igua
thuguma	urinate	imagine	gwIciria
thuura	choose	instruct	rutana
tUma	send	knead	kanda
Uka	come	lean on	komera
uma	go out	learn	kwirUta
ungania	collect	lend	kombera
ura	ooze out	lift up	oyana igUrU
		listen	thikIrIria
		look at	rora
		look for	gucaria
		migrate	thama
		ooze out	ita

Verbs (English - Kikuyu)

		penetrate	inglra thIini
		pick up	oyana igUrU
		pile up	hUmba
add up	taranIria	press out	hiha
alter	gUcenjia	pull out	gucia
arrive	gukinya	pull up	rugama
ask for	hoya	put right	thondeka
assemble	kungania	read	thoma
avoid	girIrIria	receive	amUkIra
break wind	girIrIria rUhuho	recover	hona
bring	rehe	reject	regana
bring up	gukuria	remember	ririkana
carry	kuua	reveal	kuguuria
choose	thuura	seize	kUnyita
cohabit	inglrIna	send	tUma
collect	kungania	send away	eheria
come	Uka	sit	ikarathI
come in	inglra	smell out	kunungira
decorate	gemia	squeeze out	kuhiha
deny	kara	stir up	kuuruga
dig out	cimbUria	stop up	guthika
dig up	cimbUria	suffer	gukiririra
disappear	kurira	surpass	hItUka
examine	thima	sweep up	hata
explain	tarIria	take care	menyerera
extinguish	nyotoka	take in	kwanIrIria
get well	hona	take off	ruta
give away	heana	think	gwIciria
go back	coka	threaten	makia
go in	inglra	turn over	inamia
go out	thiI	uncover	kuguuria
grow	kumera	urinate	thuguma
grow up	gUkUra	vanquish	cinda
harmonise	gutwarana	wind up	kuogotha

Reference: Webster's Online Dictionary (www.websters-online-dictionary.org)

wrap up	oha

Nouns (Kikuyu - English)

cUcU	grandmother
fUmba	dead person
gacUmbiri	highest point
gatarU	dugout canoe
gathanda mboiro	canine tooth
gicango	copper
gIIko	spitting cobra
gIthaka	thicket
gIthUri	chest
gIthUru	chest
guka	grandfather
hiti	hyena
huho	disembodied spirit
huma	breath
hUna	whistling
huria	rhinoceros
ihUragUri	medicine man
ini	liver
iria imata	curdled milk
iru	knee
itarara	python
itigo	kidney
itina	buttocks
itumbI	egg
kangamia	bedstead
kangaUrU	scorpion
kieni	open space
kIero	thigh
kIgera	machine
kIgwa	sugar cane
kIhUni	whistling
kIimba	dead person
kIndU	thing
kIngangi	crocodile
kinya	calabash
kIura	frog
macamanio	crossroads
mahuti	hay

maithori	tears
mambarita	thatched roof
manyamaro	hardship
mata	spittle
mbari	clan
mbegu	sperm
mbogo kenyarare	tsetse fly
mbUri	goat
mIrukI	vapour
mUgeni	guest
muhaka	boundary
muhane	smallpox
mUirItu	girl
mUkamo	udder
mukebe	metal pot
mukonyo	navel
mUndU mUkUrU	old person
mUndU witU	brother
mUrUwa maitU	brother
munyongoro	millipede
murango	door
muringo	rainy season
murogi	sorcerer
mUrUwa maitU	brother
muthaiga	medicine
mUthandUkU	smallpox
mUthenya	day
mUthia	highest point
mUthiIne	movement
mUthita	penis
muthonge	hut
mUtI	haft
mUtumumu	blind person
mwaka	year
mwana	child
ndegwa	heifer
ndigiri	donkey
Nganga	guinea fowl
ngarI	leopard
ngIma	monk
ngobe	eyelash
ngoma	evil spirit
ngombo	bond servant
ng'ondu	sheep
ngu	clothes
ngUkU	hen
ngwaci	sweet potato

Reference: Webster's Online Dictionary (www.websters-online-dictionary.org)

nja	courtyard	bile	nyongo
njambe	rooster	blind person	mUtumumu
njau	calf	bond servant	ngombo
njegeke	armpit	boundary	muhaka
njIra	highway	breath	huma
njora	sword	brother	mUndU witU
nUgU	monk	buttermilk	thagi
nyama	meat	buttocks	itina
nyee	testicle	calabash	kinya
nyitIro	haft	calf	njau
nyongo	bile	canine tooth	gathanda mboiro
nyUmU	dry land	cattle	uniu
nyUngU	vessel	chest	gIthUri
riko	kitchen	child	mwana
rUbutu	eyebrow	clan	mbari
rUgiri	enclosure	clothes	ngu
rUkobe	eyelash	copper	gicango
rwara	fingernail	courtyard	nja
tata	aunt	crocodile	kIngangi
tene	old times	crossroads	macamanio
thaburia	vessel	curdled milk	iria imata
thagi	buttermilk	day	mUthenya
theerI	monk	daytime	muthenya
thIna	hardship	dead person	fUmba
ucUrU	gruel	disembodied spirit	huho
UgUta	idleness	donkey	ndigiri
Uiru	jealousy	door	murango
uniu	cattle	dry land	nyUmU
urImi	agriculture	dugout canoe	gatarU
Urio	right hand	egg	itumbI
urogi	witchcraft	enclosure	rUgiri
uthayo	idleness	evil spirit	ngoma
uthondeki	medicine	eyebrow	rUbutu
wambui micore	zebra	eyelash	ngobe
		fingernail	rwara
		fireplace	riko
		firewood	ngU
		frog	kIura
		girl	mUirItu
		goat	mbUri

Nouns (English - Kikuyu)

		grandfather	guka
		grandmother	cUcU
		gruel	ucUrU
agriculture	urImi	guest	mUgeni
armpit	njegeke	guinea fowl	Nganga
aunt	tata	haft	mUtI
bedstead	kangamia	hardship	thIna
bifurcation	macamanio	hay	mahuti

hearth	riko	thigh	kIero
heifer	ndegwa	thing	kIndU
hen	ngUkU	tobacco pipe	gIIko
highest point	mUthia	tsetse fly	mbogo kenyarare
highway	njIra	udder	mUkamo
hut	muthonge	vapour	mIrukI
hyena	hiti	vessel	thaburia
idleness	UgUta	whistling	hUna
jealousy	Uiru	witchcraft	urogi
kidney	itigo	year	mwaka
kitchen	riko	zebra	wambui micore
knee	iru		
leopard	ngarI		
liver	ini		
machine	kIgera		
meat	nyama		

Adjectives (Kikuyu - English)

medicine	muthaiga		
medicine man	ihUragUri		
metal pot	mukebe		
millipede	munyongoro	**agana**	wicked
monk	ngIma	**kUra**	old
movement	mUthiIne	**kwagana**	wicked
navel	mukonyo	**mUrio**	pleasant
old person	mUndU mUkUrU	**ngUru**	old
old times	tene	**njIthi**	unripe
open space	kieni	**wIru**	ripe
penis	mUthita		
python	itarara		
rainy season	muringo		
rhinoceros	huria		
right hand	Urio		
rooster	njambe	## Adjectives (English - Kikuyu)	
scorpion	kangaUrU		
sheep	ng'ondu		
sloth	UgUta	**old**	ngUru
smallpox	mUthandUkU	**pleasant**	mUrio
sorcerer	murogi	**ripe**	wIru
sperm	mbegu	**uncooked**	njIthi
spitting cobra	gIIko	**unripe**	njIthi
spittle	mata	**wicked**	kwagana
sugar cane	kIgwa		
sweet potato	ngwaci		
sword	njora		
tears	maithori		
testicle	nyee		
thatched roof	mambarita		
thicket	gIthaka		

Index